QUILTERS PLUS

A World of Quilts

PROJECTS USING
ETHNIC FABRICS

Ethnic

Martingale®
& COMPANY

Dedication

❋ My deepest thanks to my wonderful husband and partner in an amazing journey, John, and to our terrific daughters, Caryl Elisabeth and Connor Marie. You make this all possible.

Acknowledgments

❋ Many thanks go to my friends and colleagues who contributed their time and talents to this book: Debra Becker, Carolyn Eary (who not only sewed but cooked!), Mary Kuras, Nancy Roelfsema, Kerry Steinberg, and, of course, the dedicated people at Martingale.

❋ To the folks at Grand Quilt Company: Adrienne Alexander, Karen Beaman, Linda Bennett, Julie Bennison, Susie Breen, Susan Cortese, Ruth DeJager, Carolyn Eary, Estella Fessenden, Ginger Hoop, Kathy Johnson, Deb Kuhns, Amy Sprik, Nancy and Keith Roelfsema, Laurie and Ashlee Vance, Lori and Verlyn Verbrugge, and Deb Wisneski—thanks for making Grand Quilt such a wonderful place to teach (and hang out!) when I'm not on the road. You're great!

❋ To Sue and Mike Callihan—thank you for your constant friendship, support, and encouragement.

❋ To Diane Peffer, Mary Kuras, Roxann Shier, Cindy Rowe, Mary Taylor, and Connie Young—thank you for your patience and understanding when I'm in "survival mode." Your friendship is a blessing I treasure. And to my mothers and sisters, Carol King, Jennifer King, Amy Logsdon, Sue Williams, Barbara Williams, and Heather Williams—thank you for everything you are to me.

A World of Quilts:
10 Projects Using Ethnic Fabrics
© 2003 by Beth Ann Williams

That Patchwork Place® is an imprint
of Martingale & Company®.

Martingale & Company
20205 144th Avenue NE
Woodinville, WA 98072-8478
www.martingale-pub.com

CREDITS

President: Nancy J. Martin
CEO: Daniel J. Martin
Publisher: Jane Hamada
Editorial Director: Mary V. Green
Managing Editor: Tina Cook
Technical Editor: Cyndi Hershey
Copy Editor: Melissa Bryan
Design Director: Stan Green
Illustrator: Robin Strobel
Cover and Text Designer: Regina Girard
Photographer: Brent Kane

MISSION STATEMENT
*Dedicated to providing quality products
and service to inspire creativity.*

Printed in China
08 07 06 05 04 03   8 7 6 5 4 3 2 1

Library of Congress Cataloging-in-Publication Data
Williams, Beth Ann.
   A world of quilts : 10 projects using ethnic fabrics / Beth Ann Williams.
      p. cm.
   ISBN 1-56477-504-6
   1. Quilting—Patterns. 2. Patchwork—Patterns.
3. Multiculturalism in art. I. Title.
   TT835 .W5349 2003
   746.46'041—dc21

2003008961

CONTENTS

INTRODUCTION

I often joke that when it comes to fabric, I am an equal-opportunity spender. That is, I love color, pattern, and texture, and like most quilters I am apt to find must-have fabrics wherever I go. Distinctive fabrics may show up at your local quilt shop, or you might bring them home as wonderful souvenirs of special trips or friendships. Fabrics enrich our personal spaces, providing visual cues that link us to exotic locales or to familiar historical or cultural symbols.

For the purposes of this book, we'll focus on 100%-cotton quilting-weight fabrics, since they tend to be easiest to work with and most readily available to quilters. My approach to fabric sources, on the other hand, is rather eclectic. Some of the fabrics in this book have been imported directly from Africa, Asia (most notably Japan), India, Australia, Indonesia, and the South Pacific. Other fabrics were produced by various North American and European manufacturers in the style of or inspired by authentic ethnic textiles and designs. Both the availability and the price range of certain fabrics can vary dramatically from region to region. If you have any difficulty locating the fabrics you need in your local quilt shop (or you just want to browse through some wonderful collections!), you may find the addresses, phone numbers, and Web sites I have listed in the "Resources" section to be very helpful. Combining fabrics from a variety of sources, both international and domestic, can make these exciting looks easier to achieve without sacrificing anything in terms of quality or beauty. Personally, I also find a multicultural approach very appealing, since it so vividly reflects not only the rich social diversity of our world today, but my own history of living on three continents—each of which has left its mark on my heart and soul.

As a special feature, I've tried to share in this book a bit of the relevant cultural background for many of the fabrics shown. Space limitations preclude in-depth explorations of the fascinating history and symbolism often found in traditional fabrics from around the world, but I hope I've included enough to whet your appetite and convey my own appreciation for the stories we can tell through our fabric choices.

You will notice that although some of the projects look a bit complex, the sewing techniques used are really quite simple and streamlined, relying on rotary cutting, straight-seam machine sewing, and machine quilting. A few of the projects involve adaptations of familiar, traditional quilt blocks such as Log Cabin and Fence Rail. Visual complexity comes from the richness of the fabrics used, not from intricate piecework or complex processes. These projects are designed to be assembled quickly and easily even by those who may be new to quilting. For those of you trying to fit your sewing and quilting time into busy schedules filled with family, career, or community commitments, take heart. Let the fabric do most of the work!

TIP

Many quilt shops, quilting catalogs, and Web sites have fat quarter clubs or programs that you can join to receive an automatic monthly or bimonthly shipment of fat quarters of a particular type of fabric. These programs are a great way to build up your fabric stash—and it's terrific fun to open the packages and discover what new treasures have arrived!

Fabric, a.k.a. Around the World in 80 Bolts

In this section, I'd like to share with you a brief overview of quilting-weight cotton fabrics from various parts of the world. We'll also look at some suggestions you might find helpful when working with these exciting fabrics.

AUSTRALIAN

The Australian fabrics used in this book are distributed by Leo9 Textiles. These fascinating designs are by well-known Aboriginal artists from Central Australia and the Northern Territory such as Linda Meyers, Sarah Nelson, Nicole Postema, and Reggie Sutan. Each fabric tells a story, many of which are Dreamtime stories, embodying both cultural transmission and spiritual significance. Some of the symbols are in widespread use throughout the region, while others are unique to the individual artist.

Fabrics Designed by Australian Aboriginal Artists

AFRICAN

The African fabrics in this book reflect many different countries as well as a variety of possible production techniques, such as wax printing, screen printing, and roller printing. A few fabrics might actually have been produced elsewhere for the African market, but most were printed in West or Central Africa and imported into the United States by Homeland Fabrics.

You'll notice that African prints tend to be extremely bold and dramatic in both color and scale; this makes perfect sense when you think about the glare of the African sun and the magnitude of the landscape. Many African cottons feature layouts and traditional motifs from African woven, resist-dyed, embroidered, block-printed, and/or dyed textiles. Textiles most often imitated include Kente cloth, mudcloth (also called Bogolan or Bogolanfini), Kuba cloth, Adinkra, and Adire cloth. Some African prints feature a crackled appearance imitating Javanese batiks, which have been popular since they were introduced in some parts of Africa by European (especially Dutch) traders during the seventeenth century or brought back by West African soldiers returning from military campaigns in Indonesia in the nineteenth century. Whether printed, woven, or embroidered, the patterns in African textiles often tell stories or proverbs that illustrate family and community values.

Fabrics from West and Central Africa

Fabrics Inspired by African Textiles and Themes

ASIAN

Many of the fabrics shown in this book were imported directly from Japan. Authentic Japanese fabrics are increasingly available in the United States, both in vintage pieces (often in the form of kimonos or obis) and in new yardage. I have not attempted to represent the full range of imported quilting-weight cottons from Japan (or from any other country!), but I have selected some of my personal favorites. I've also used some of the wonderful Japanese- and Chinese-inspired cotton fabrics produced specifically for the quilting market.

Vintage Kimono Fabrics from Katie's Vintage Kimono

Japanese Indigo Fabrics from Hanamomen

Japanese Multicolored Cottons from Hanamomen

Asian-Style Prints

INDONESIAN

Although batik seems to have originated in China or India, possibly as early as the fourth or fifth century C.E., and is found in various forms all over the world, it is widely considered to have reached its highest form of artistic expression in Indonesia.

Generally, batik is a process of using a resist, usually wax, to create or add additional detail to a design, followed by immersing the fabric in a dye bath. The intricate patterning of Tulis batik, the oldest form of production, is created by hand application of wax to the fabric with a pen-like tool called a tjanting. Once the wax has been applied, the fabric is treated with the first dye. Then a second coat of wax is added, covering portions of the design that are meant to remain the first color. The fabric is then dyed with the second color. Subsequent colors are added in the same manner and the full design is gradually revealed.

Copper-stamp batik evolved in the mid-1800s out of a commercial need to speed up and simplify production. A tjap, or stamp, is used to apply the wax in a regular repeat pattern. Today, a silk-screen process creates many of the modern Indonesian batiks.

Historically, textiles have served as a major source of communication and visual expression throughout the many islands that make up Indonesia. The center of Indonesian batik production is Java, although even within Java there are distinct regional differences in style and pattern.

Batiks from Bali are quite familiar to quilting-catalog aficionados in the United States. However, beautiful batiks continue to be produced throughout Indonesia, the South Pacific, and even in India and Africa. Many of these gorgeous fabrics feature strong colorations—the colors may appear to be layered or mottled, and value contrasts can vary from subtle to extreme. Motifs are regularly spaced and may range from delicately ornate to boldly graphic.

Batik Fabrics in a Variety of Colors and Scales

Individual blocks or hand-painted landscapes, animals, masks, and other motifs are becoming increasingly available (and popular!). A large scene makes a great focal point for a quilt, while smaller blocks can add great interest to the overall composition. Cultural borrowing seems to be very popular with the artists—while some designs are clearly Indonesian in flavor, others may be African or Asian, as in the case of the Ghanian symbols used in "Adinkra Pillow" on page 52.

Slightly more subdued colorations and finely detailed allover patterns are evident in the selection of wonderfully soft cotton sarongs of both vintage and modern Indonesian batik shown at right and below.

TIP

Since both sides of batik fabrics are fully printed or dyed, there is usually no right or wrong side for you to use.

Scenic and Theme Blocks in Hand-Painted Batiks

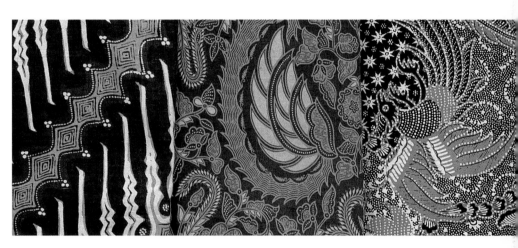

Vintage Cotton Sarongs Featuring Indonesian Batiks

More Cotton-Sarong Fabrics

COMPANION FABRICS

You will notice that I generally don't hesitate to place visually rich prints next to each other—I tend not to worry about fabrics being too busy to be used in combination. I adore the blending that occurs when similar visual textures are combined, especially when the pairing is used to disguise rigid seam lines and create impressions of unified color and light. However, there are times when overall strength or "readability" requires a visual break between design elements. A gorgeous print or scenic panel becomes the center of attention it deserves to be when surrounded with comparatively quieter fabrics. Slightly mottled or subtle prints make it easier to show off your piecing skills or emphasize interesting shapes. However, I usually prefer to avoid solid fabrics, finding them overly stark.

UNITY VS. DIVERSITY

Although I've occasionally been accused of throwing in everything but the kitchen sink, I always follow certain unifying principles when combining fabrics. A certain amount of diversity is highly desirable, but too much can lead to visual chaos. Look for similarities in color, value, saturation/intensity, visual texture, or pattern character (the scale, type of motif, etc.) to relate or tie together fabrics from different sources. Repeated design elements, scales, values, or colors will help give your creation a unified fabric palette.

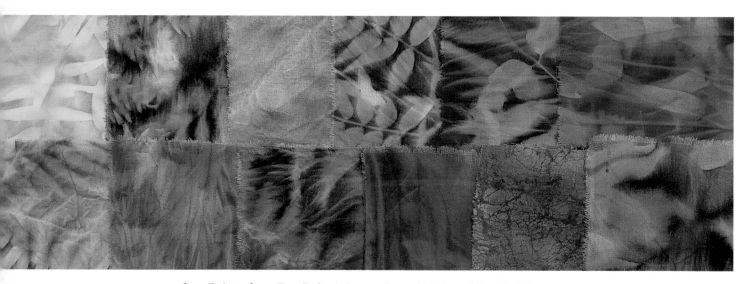

Sun Prints from Pru Bolus's Langa Lapu Fabrics of South Africa

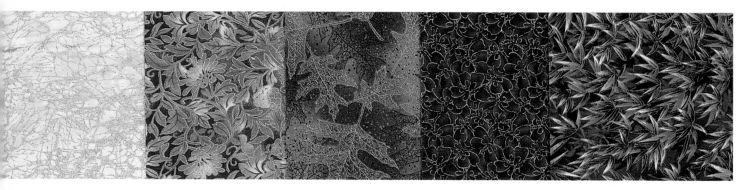

Smaller-Scale Textured Prints That Complement Large-Scale Asian and Asian-Influenced Fabrics

The suggested combinations that follow will hopefully help you take advantage of fabrics that may seem harder to use because of their unfamiliar nature:

Hand-dyed or hand-painted fabrics (or commercial prints designed to imitate the hand-dyed or hand-painted effect) can make wonderful solids to use with deeply saturated prints. Langa Lapu Fabrics produces a wonderful line of 60"-wide sun-printed fabrics that I especially enjoy using.

Vivid batiks tend to combine well with the bold graphics of African fabrics; more toned (dusky and muted) batiks work well with many Aboriginal designs. Asian fabrics can also be combined with batiks, although I suggest in most cases sticking with subtle prints or mottled painterly batiks. However, the fine detail and medium to large scale of sarong batiks can be quite compatible with many other Asian or Indonesian fabrics.

Geometrics (with or without metallic accents) and animal prints provide a striking complement to the bold lines and graphic nature of many African prints.

Subtle tone-on-tone and textured prints can complement the bold patterns but slightly softened colors of Australian Aboriginal fabrics.

Textured prints (with or without metallic accents) and prints with subtle tone-on-tone appeal can also be combined wonderfully with large-scale Asian prints.

Fun Types of Fabrics to Combine with African Prints

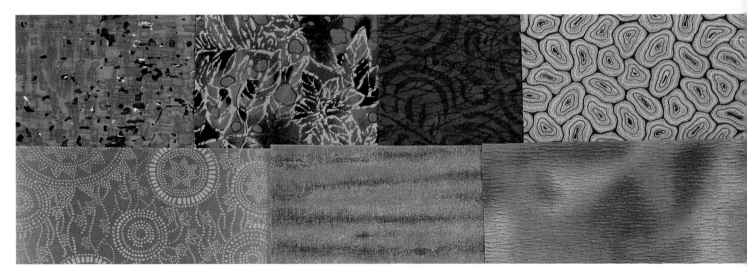

Fabrics That Combine Well with Aboriginal Prints

To Prewash or Not to Prewash?

Sometimes it seems you can find as many answers to this question as you find quilters. For the projects I discuss in this book, however, the answer seems very clear.

Since it is important to me to be able to launder my finished projects in the washer and dryer without risking ruination, I always wash all my fabrics before using them. While price points can serve as a general indicator of quality, even high-end quilting fabrics can bleed or shrink in unexpected ways! And when buying international fabrics, you will find that many of the importers and/or distributors will even include prewashing instructions with your fabric order.

One issue concerns the variables of fillers, thread count, and shrinkage. Although cotton is generally considered a stable fiber, the looseness of the weave itself can cause a given fabric to shrink considerably, sometimes more in one direction than another. A loose weave or flimsy hand may be camouflaged by the addition of fillers that temporarily stiffen the fabric. When you wash the fabric, the fillers disappear and the true nature of the fabric is revealed. It is much better to find this out beforehand than after it is too late to remove the fabric from your project! Even in quilts only a few years old, we often find that one or more fabrics are wearing out much sooner than the other fabrics in the quilt. (This phenomenon is even more evident in antique quilts.) If you find yourself with a fabric that turns out to be much flimsier than you expected, I suggest that you back it with lightweight fusible interfacing to bring it up to the weight of the other fabrics you are using, or simply set it aside for another use.

Another extremely important consideration is colorfastness, as well as the separate (but related) issue of excess dye. Generally speaking, deep reds, purples, and blues seem to be the most likely to bleed. However, I have found that even high-quality fabrics of almost any color may contain excess dye.

I like to use a product called Retayne to set the dye of any fabric that I suspect might bleed. Rarely, I find a fabric that continues to bleed when I swish a piece in warm water, even after it has been treated one or more times to set the dye. There comes a point when you are better off simply not using that fabric, however beautiful it might be. For the majority of fabrics, however, the issue is not so much that the dyes are not fast, but that there is simply too much dye in the fabric, and not all of the dye was absorbed. This dye needs to be rinsed out so that it cannot turn up later somewhere it does not belong. I have been very pleased with both Shout Color Catcher and Woolite Dye Magnet sheets, which you put into the wash cycle with your fabric. These products are designed to absorb the excess dye in the wash water before the dye can be redeposited. Synthrapol is a mild detergent used by hand dyers that serves the same purpose.

To sum up: What works best for me is to set deep dyes with Retayne (no other detergent necessary). To wash the rest of my fabrics, I first sort them into lights, mediums, and darks (like laundry!), wash them in slightly warm water with a color-absorbing product, and follow that with a cool-water rinse.

Look at Your Fabrics in New Ways!

Open up your fabric yardage to consider the full impact of large-scale motifs or scenic prints. Then form a 2" viewing window with your fingers and move your hands over the fabric, isolating small portions of the design. This will make it easier for you to observe the visual texture of the fabric: Are the lines mostly straight, curvy, or mixed? Is there high contrast or low contrast between the colors? What is the overall impression?

Sometimes I like to take advantage of one or more large pictorial elements by making them the major focus of the design; other times I prefer to emphasize the exciting interaction of color and visual texture when smaller pieces of these wonderful fabrics are combined. When a particular print so captivates me that I am loathe to cut it up, I like to use it as a backing fabric—making the quilt reversible (see "Shield" on page 38).

What about All Those Strings?

Before you put your wet fabrics into the dryer, take the time to straighten out each piece, and clip any long strings that might be dangling. If the fabric goes into the dryer smooth, it will likely come out smooth. If it goes in a crumpled mess—you guessed it, yuck! You can reduce the fraying of the cut edges by trimming a small triangle from each corner of the fabric, or by my favorite method, using a rotary cutter with a wave blade to pink the edges. (Pinking shears also work; they just take longer.) In extreme cases, you might find it helpful to serge or zigzag the cut edges before laundering the fabric, but I rarely find that necessary.

QUANTITIES AND FAT QUARTERS

The yardage requirements for the projects in this book assume 42"-wide fabric (unless using fat quarters, as you'll find out shortly), with a usable width of 40" after washing. However, some imported fabrics may be slightly wider or narrower than this. If that is the case with the fabric(s) you have selected, you might need slightly more or less fabric than I've listed for a particular project. Directional designs (such as stripes) or specific motifs that you plan to fussy cut may also require additional fabric and/or a change in the cutting instructions.

As you look over the projects in this book, you'll repeatedly come across the designation "Fat quarter friendly!" A fat quarter is a quarter yard of fabric cut approximately 18" x 22", as opposed to a quarter yard cut selvage to selvage, which is approximately 9" x 44". I find fat quarters to be more convenient to wash, store, and use than long quarters. I also find that both individual fat quarters and sampler packs of fat quarters offer quick and easy ways to broaden my fabric stash without breaking my budget.

When using fat quarters instead of fabric cut selvage to selvage, it is important to orient the fat quarter so that you are cutting the longest strips you can; ideally the strips should be 20" to 22" long. Generally speaking, you will need to cut twice as many strips from a fat quarter than will be specified in the project directions. As a result, if you are combining these strips with strips that were cut selvage to selvage, you will need to cut the longer strips in half to match the fat quarter strips. As an example, instead of sewing one long strip set, you would be sewing two short strip sets.

Equipment and Supplies

I find that using the right equipment and supplies makes my life as a quilter much easier and much more enjoyable. The following are items that I find work best for me, but please feel free to use whatever suits you best.

SEWING MACHINE

All the projects in this book were assembled by machine. With the exception of the bed quilts that were quilted on long-arm machines, all were also machine quilted on regular home sewing machines. For piecing, you will need to be able to sew a perfectly straight seam with a very consistent seam allowance. For machine quilting, you might also need to know how to change the presser feet, increase or decrease the tension setting for the top thread, raise and lower the feed dogs (if applicable to your machine), and adjust the pressure on the presser foot.

It is important that you diligently maintain your sewing machine, keeping it oiled (if appropriate) and cleaned regularly. Lint and debris can build up very quickly, especially in the tension discs, around the presser bar and needle bar, under the needle plate, and around the bobbin area. Treat your machine kindly and it will do the same for you!

PRESSER FEET

Quarter-Inch Foot: Many people find a quarter-inch foot invaluable for piecing with consistently accurate seam allowances. A word of caution, however: some quarter-inch feet actually create a seam allowance that is slightly larger than ¼" when the seam allowance has been pressed to one side. This can make intersections much more difficult to match. If that is the case, try moving your needle to the right position (instead of center) or simply attempt to keep your seam allowance a thread or two narrower than the edge of the foot.

Walking Foot/Even-Feed Foot/Plaid Matcher: The walking foot, also known as the even-feed foot or plaid matcher, is a unique attachment in that it allows multiple layers of fabric (or the layers of a quilt sandwich: quilt top, batting, and backing) to move through the machine at an even rate, minimizing shifting. It does this by reproducing the action of the feed dogs below the fabric on the top layer (or layers) of fabric. This foot can be helpful for piecing and is absolutely indispensable for machine-guided machine quilting.

If possible, use the walking foot designed especially for your machine. If you cannot find your brand, try a generic walking foot. Make sure that the feeders (also called teeth or grippers) inside the foot align exactly with the feed dogs on your sewing machine. If they do not, the fabric will not feed properly and you may be worse off than if you had no walking foot at all!

Note: If your machine has built-in dual feed, you do not need a walking foot.

Darning/Free-Motion/Spring Embroidery Foot: The darning foot, also known as the free-motion foot or spring embroidery foot, is another attachment that not only goes by a variety of names, but once again can vary dramatically in appearance from one brand to another. This special foot gives you the ability to move the fabric freely from side to side and back to front as you sew. The foot itself moves up and down with the needle. When the needle is up, you can steer the fabric in any direction. When the needle is down, the foot descends to hold the fabric firmly against the machine's throat plate so that a proper stitch can be formed. This foot is vital for free-motion quilting.

Open-Toe Appliqué Foot: This foot has a large opening in front of the needle, which allows for better visibility when you are stitching. It also has a groove on the bottom so that stitches can pass easily underneath. You can substitute a satin-stitch foot or zigzag foot, although visibility may not be quite as good.

SEWING-MACHINE NEEDLES

Choosing an appropriate size and type of needle is an often-overlooked step in piecing and machine quilting, but it can make an amazing difference in the end results. Unlike thread, which gets smaller in diameter as the weight or size number increases, needles get larger as the size number increases.

Needles also vary in terms of the shape of the point, the size and shape of the eye, and the contours of the needle shaft. All these characteristics are engineered to work best with particular combinations of fabric and thread.

Change Your Needle Often!

Please don't wait until your needle breaks before you change it. Wisps of thread or batting poking through the quilt, skipped or irregular stitches, breaking thread, or an odd popping sound when the needle hits the fabric (snagging or punching through the layers instead of gliding through) can all be signs that it is time for a new needle. I change mine every other time I change my bobbin—and clean out my machine at the same time.

Sharps: Sometimes labeled Microtex Sharps, these needles have a very sharp point and a narrow eye, allowing them to pierce cleanly and create a very small hole. This, in turn, helps keep the bobbin thread from popping through to the front of your work. I like to use size 70 Sharps for machine piecing, especially when working with tightly woven fabrics such as batiks, since the fineness of the needle makes it easier to create perfectly straight seams. (Sometimes tightly woven threads can force a duller or thicker needle slightly off to the side instead of allowing it to slide neatly through.) The size 70 is also my favorite choice for invisible machine appliqué and for quilting with .004 monofilament, although it is not as strong as the quilting needle and therefore more susceptible to breakage.

Quilting Needles: Quilting needles were developed especially for quiltmaking and feature a strong, reinforced shaft and sharp, tapered point. I often use a size 75 quilting needle for piecing. It is also one of my top choices for machine quilting or appliqué with .004 monofilament, 50- or 60-weight mercerized cotton thread, or 40-weight rayon thread. I reserve the size 90 (which makes a considerably larger hole) for machine quilting with 30- to 40-weight mercerized cotton thread or 30- to 35-weight rayon thread.

If you can find one small enough, either a jeans needle or a topstitching needle can be a good alternative.

Embroidery Needles: Embroidery needles were designed to handle the often-delicate threads used for machine embroidery and decorative stitching. The eye is large and the scarf, which is the indentation behind the eye, is modified to reduce friction on threads that may have a tendency to fray or split. This is my favorite needle for machine quilting with rayon thread, especially when I am using a decorative stitch, such as in "Asian Fans Table Runner" on page 62.

I like to use sizes 75 and 90, with the needle size depending on the weight of the thread.

Choose your needle size according to the thread you are using. A fine thread should be matched with a fine needle. If too large a needle is used, you end up with a perforated quilt since the thread cannot adequately fill the holes created by the large needle. A needle that's too small causes excessive friction on a heavy thread and may lead to fraying or breakage.

THREAD

Size .004 Monofilament: For invisible machine appliqué (as described on page 22) as well as certain machine-quilting techniques, you'll probably wish to use monofilament thread in either clear or smoke. The clear monofilament is best for fabrics in light to medium color values, or dark fabrics printed with light motifs. The smoke-colored monofilament is appropriate for very dark fabrics where it is easily hidden. Size .004 monofilament may be made of nylon or polyester. I find that the nylon monofilament has a little more stretch and seems to work better in my machine. However, I've also found that other machines sometimes prefer the polyester monofilament. Either way, the thread should be marked .004 and should be very fine, soft, and stretchy—nothing like the fishing-line invisible thread still sold in many stores.

If you experience difficulty with monofilament sliding off the end of the spool and becoming wrapped around the spool pin, you will be much happier if you can switch to a vertical spool position and/or use a thread net to keep the thread from coiling off the spool as you work. Don't be afraid to experiment with your upper thread tension when you use monofilament; some machines require no adjustment at all, while others require dramatic changes in the upper thread tension setting.

Mercerized Cotton: I always use 50-weight, 3-ply mercerized cotton thread (silk finish or long-staple fiber types) for piecing. (You'll generally find this information either written out or abbreviated as 50/3 on the end of the spool. If your thread is not marked, it is usually about 50-weight, which is

considered an all-purpose size.) For machine appliqué I like 60-weight, 2-ply mercerized cotton thread (machine-embroidery weight) since it is finer and more able to sink down into the fabric, creating a less visible stitch. Either weight yields satisfying results when machine quilting, although the 50-weight thread will be stronger.

Slightly heavier yet, and therefore stronger, 30- to 40-weight thread can also be a good choice for machine quilting, particularly when the quilting lines will be widely spaced.

Rayon: While rayon thread is not heavy duty enough to use for piecing or for machine quilting of projects that will be washed frequently, I love the rich color and subtle shine rayon thread adds to wall hangings or decorative pieces that will not see hard use. I most often select a 40-weight (sometimes indicated by No. 40 on the end of the spool) variegated thread. Some brands of rayon have a much looser twist than others and seem to fray or break more frequently. You may wish to try a couple different kinds to determine which you prefer.

Note: I do not recommend using monofilament or rayon thread in your bobbin. Instead, I use 50- or 60-weight mercerized cotton in the bobbin, selecting a color (or colors) that will blend with my quilt top and/or my backing fabric.

ROTARY-CUTTING EQUIPMENT

Rotary Cutter: A number of different rotary-cutter models are available, some more comfortable to use than others. It's worth taking the time to determine which is your favorite. A relatively recent innovation is the Ergo rotary cutter, designed to reduce stress on your hand and wrist—especially helpful for combating carpal tunnel syndrome. Another advantage of this model is that you can rotary cut while seated.

Cutting Mat: I recommend a gridded cutting mat at least 24" x 36" (the printed grid may be 23" x 35"). Check the grid on your mat against the grid on your rotary ruler; they should match up exactly.

Acrylic Ruler: Your acrylic ruler should be at least 24" long. I find a 6" x 24" size ideal.

PRESSING ESSENTIALS

A good, clean steam iron may be helpful when blocking finished projects, although I don't recommend using steam during the construction of your project. I find that a dry iron is less likely to cause stretching and distortion.

The Clover Mini Iron is wonderful for pressing seam allowances over the edges of freezer-paper templates when preparing shapes for invisible machine appliqué. The small size provides excellent visibility while you work, and the lighter weight is much easier on your arm than a full-sized iron. The product does get extremely hot, though, so use caution. I never turn mine all the way to the highest setting; closer to medium heat seems to work well.

A standard ironing board works just fine for most purposes. However, when you need a very crisp edge, such as when preparing shapes for appliqué, your board's padding might not provide the firm resistance needed. I've discovered that an empty fabric bolt from the quilt shop or fabric store is ideal—and usually free for the asking.

ASSORTED NOTIONS

Scissors or Thread Snips: Thread snips or other small scissors are great for clipping threads as you work.

Seam Ripper: A seam ripper is invaluable for "sewing in reverse"—necessary from time to time.

Safety Pins: I like the medium (size 2, or 1½" long) safety pins for pin-basting the quilt sandwich in preparation for machine quilting. Be sure to use pins that are sharp and fine enough to penetrate the fabric easily without snagging or pulling.

Straight Pins: Unfortunately, many so-called quilting pins can actually be quite harmful to your project—too blunt and too large in diameter, they can end up leaving holes or snags in the fabric. I have been very happy with the IBC (Imported by Clotilde) 1⅜" glass-head silk pins, which have a .50-mm shaft.

Value Finder: A value finder, such as the Ruby Beholder®, is a red filter usually made of either acetate or acrylic. Viewing a selection of fabrics through the red filter visually cancels out the color

of the fabrics, thus simplifying the process of determining the fabrics' relative value. This is particularly helpful when trying to create an illusion such as the diagonal stair-stepping across the face of the "Japanese Indigos" quilt on page 44; because all the fabrics were indigo and cream, it was sometimes difficult to determine if a given fabric would work better as a light/medium or as a medium/dark. Looking at the final arrangement through a Ruby Beholder helped me evaluate whether I had created the effect I was looking for.

Low-Tack Masking Tape: I often use low-tack masking tape (such as you use when painting a room) to label sections of my project. This helps me stay organized—and averts potential disaster when Chester and Charlie (our sometimes overly affectionate cats) sneak into my quilting studio.

Freezer Paper: American-style freezer paper has a waxy coating (actually made of plastic) on one side, which makes it wonderful for easily preparing shapes for invisible machine appliqué. It is widely available in grocery stores (especially during hunting season!) as well as in many quilt shops and catalogs.

BATTING

I highly favor a low-loft cotton or cotton-blend batting for softness, drape, texture, and ease of machine quilting. Almost all the projects in this book were made with Hobbs Heirloom Premium batting, an 80% cotton–20% polyester blend. This batting is also newly available in a fusible version, which I have found quite wonderful to work with.

It is important to read the package to determine if you should wash a particular batting before using it, and also to find out how densely it needs to be quilted. Many manufacturers, retailers, quilt catalogs, and machine-quilting books offer charts listing the relative properties of various batting types. Compare for yourself, and use what you like!

General Instructions

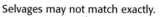

Although the rich fabrics in this book make for visually exciting projects, you'll probably be surprised to realize how easy most of these techniques really are. The key is to take each process step by step, don't rush, and stay organized. If you can rotary cut a straight strip and sew a straight seam with a consistent seam allowance, you can do this!

WHATEVER WORKS!

I try to share with you here the methods that work best for me; however, everyone has her or his own work style, so if another approach is better for you, by all means, feel free to experiment!

ROTARY CUTTING

In most cases, the directions for each project will tell you first how many strips to cut, and then how to subcut those strips into the pieces you'll need (for some other projects you'll use templates). The initial strips should always be cut selvage to selvage if you are using the full width of your yardage, or parallel to the longest edge (approximately 21" to 22") if you are using fat quarters.

1. Prewash all your fabrics and press, if needed.

2. On your cutting mat, fold your fabric in half, selvage to selvage. (Due to distortion in the manufacturing process, the selvages may not always line up exactly.) When you make the first

fold, line up the fold with a grid line on your cutting mat. Try to fold the fabric along the grain line. Don't let yourself be overly distracted by the print on the fabric; many fabrics (especially those from Africa) are printed at least slightly off grain. Just make sure the fabric lies smooth and flat, with no pulls or wrinkles along the fold.

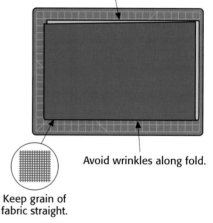

Selvages may not match exactly.

Avoid wrinkles along fold.

Keep grain of fabric straight.

3. If you are using the full width of your yardage, fold the fabric a second time so that the first fold lines up with the selvages. This second fold should follow the grain line of the fabric and the grid lines on the cutting mat in the same way as the first fold.

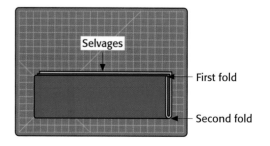

Selvages

First fold

Second fold

4. Trim the left edge (or right edge if you are left-handed) as shown.

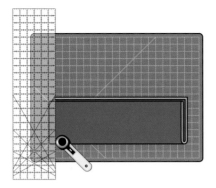

5. Measure in from the trimmed edge and cut a strip to the width specified in the pattern instructions. Unfold the strip to make certain it is straight (see illustration at top of page 20). If the strip is crooked or uneven, adjust the fold of the fabric. Cut the number of strips.

6. Turn the strips sideways, trim, and subcut as directed.

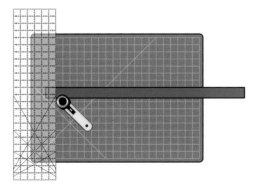

Note: If you are strip piecing, you will not make the subcuts until the strip-pieced panels have been completely sewn.

Always walk your hand up the ruler as you cut. If you plant your hand in the middle of the ruler, it is much more likely to pivot slightly as you cut, resulting in strips with uneven edges.

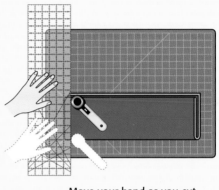

Move your hand as you cut.

SEWING STRIP SETS

I must begin this section with a word of caution: Joining fabrics from a variety of sources can produce wonderfully rich and complex combinations. However, care must be taken when combining fabrics that vary in thread count or tightness of the weave. Some will have more stretch than others and may become slightly distorted during sewing and pressing, even if they were accurately cut. The sewing and pressing suggestions in this section will help you avoid unhappy surprises!

To help minimize stretching and distortion, I like to join pairs of strips and then pairs of pairs. As you press each pair of strips, be sure to press the seam allowances in the direction given in the project instructions.

1. Lay out your fabric strips in the order in which they will be sewn. Before you sew a strip, check the edges and use the strip only if the edges are

quite straight; avoid using strips that are crooked or uneven.

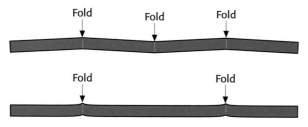

Don't use strips with crooked or uneven edges.

2. With small pieces of low-tack masking tape, label each strip with its correct sewing-order number. Avoid placing the tape in the seam-allowance areas.

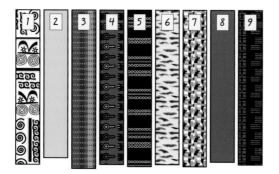

Number the strips.

3. To sew, flip strip 2 on top of strip 1 so that right sides are together; sew along the right-hand edge. Continue by sewing strip 4 on top of strip 3, and so on.

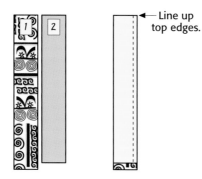

← Line up top edges.

Sewing the strips in this manner helps prevent bowed or slanted strip sets.

As you stitch the beginning and end of each seam, the fabric may have a tendency to slip to one side or another, distorting the first and last ½" of the seam. To avoid these fluctuations, I like to begin the seam on a small scrap of fabric. Then I sew "on air" for a few stitches before sliding the real fabric under the presser foot. (I do not raise the presser foot at all.) Then I end the seam the same way, with a few stitches on air followed by a scrap piece of fabric or by the next pair of strips.

Seam allowance too wide

Top corner "eaten" by machine

Seam allowance too narrow

Stitches swing off to the side at the end of the strip

4. Press carefully. It is very important to lift the iron off the fabric as you move it along the seam. Press—don't iron! In other words, don't slide the iron along the fabric because this may cause the fabric to stretch. (I avoid using steam for that reason.) To get a cleanly finished seam, press first from the back side to set the stitches.

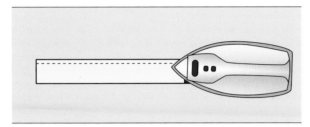

Press up and down. Don't slide the iron.

5. Next, flip the top piece over, right side up. Gently separate the strips with your fingers, making sure there are no tucks in the fabric as you press the seam to one side with the tip of your iron held at a slight sideways angle.

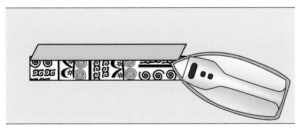

Press with tip of iron at a slight sideways angle.

Finally, press the unit once more from the right side, making sure the seam allowance is still pressed to one side. Note that each pattern will indicate the directions in which seam allowances should be pressed.

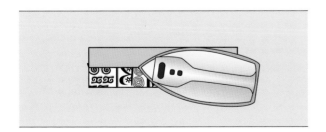

Pressing

Generally, if you are making two strip sets, you will be directed to press the seam allowances of the first set toward the first strip and the seam allowances of the second set away from the first strip. This method will allow the seams to oppose each other and neatly butt against each other (or "nest") during final assembly of the quilt top.

6. Continue sewing the pairs of strips together, pressing carefully after each round. Then join and press the strip pairs. Be sure to sew the pairs in the order in which they're numbered! The higher number always flips over onto the lower number, right sides together, and you always sew down the right-hand edge.

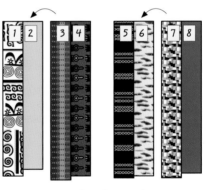

Sew strip pairs together.

Continue joining and pressing the strips until they are all sewn into one panel or complete strip set.

PIECING SINGLE UNITS

The method for sewing strip sets works equally well for assembling units such as squares or rectangles.

1. Lay out the pieces and number them, if desired.

2. Flip, sew, and press in the same manner described in steps 3–6 of the preceding section, creating rows. Press all the seam allowances in each row in the same direction and alternate the direction from row to row.

3. Sew the rows together. The seam allowances between each row should nest neatly.

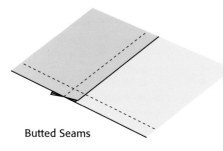

Butted Seams

INVISIBLE MACHINE APPLIQUÉ

My favorite way to prepare shapes for invisible machine appliqué is the freezer-paper method. It allows me to create sharp, well-defined edges and points and a nice flat finish.

To prepare a shape for appliqué:

1. Trace the exact shape onto the paper side of the freezer paper. Trace and cut out as many copies as needed, since each freezer-paper template will be used only once.

2. Pin the freezer-paper template paper side down on the back of your appliqué fabric.

3. Cut the shape from the fabric, adding an approximate ¼"-wide seam allowance on all sides.

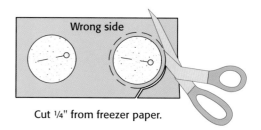

Wrong side

Cut ¼" from freezer paper.

Note: Do not add seam allowances to edges that will be flush with the edge of the background fabric. These seam allowances are already included in the templates.

4. If necessary, clip any sharp curves or corners. (Gentle curves on the bias are usually fine without clipping.)

5. With the tip of your iron, press the seam allowance of the fabric over the edge of the freezer-paper shape to the waxy side of the paper (the right side of the fabric should show when you turn the unit over). (Alternatively, you may be more comfortable using your fingernail to pull a small section of the seam allowance straight over the edge of the freezer paper and hold it there until you can catch it with the tip of the iron.) Remove the pins.

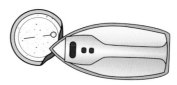

6. Press your shape into place on the background fabric. (The waxy side of the freezer paper will adhere to your backing fabric, but also secure it with a pin to be safe.)

7. Sew. (See "The Appliqué Stitch" at right.)

8. Remove the freezer paper. If your shape has an unstitched edge, you can simply reach in under this unstitched area, use your fingernail to pull the seam allowance away from the freezer paper, and pull the paper out. If your shape has no unstitched areas, you'll need to turn your work over and cut out the fabric behind your appliqué to remove the freezer paper. Be sure to leave adequate seam allowances behind the shape, and take care not to puncture the top layer when making your initial cut.

Wrong side of background

Remove freezer paper.

Alternative Methods

You could press the initial freezer-paper shape to the wrong side of the fabric (waxy side down), cut it out with seam allowances, and baste the seam allowance of the fabric to the paper side of the freezer paper with water-soluble glue stick. If your appliqué shape is directional, you would need to trace the template in reverse.

Basting the seam allowances by brushing them with liquid starch and pressing over templates made from stiff paper or card stock is also possible.

The Appliqué Stitch

There are several stitches that work very well for invisible machine appliqué. The blind-hem stitch, the buttonhole or heirloom stitch, and the zigzag stitch seem to be the most popular. You may wish to experiment to see which you prefer. My personal choice is a small zigzag stitch.

I set my sewing machine for a zigzag stitch with a width of 1.5. Sometimes I'll drop down to 1.0, but this size can be harder to see and therefore harder to control. I set the stitch length to 1.5.

Please note that stitch sizes can vary widely from machine to machine, so I suggest trying a few test swatches to determine the settings that will work best for your particular unit.

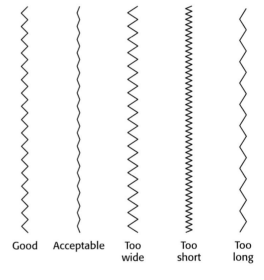

| Good | Acceptable | Too wide | Too short | Too long |

Zigzag Stitch

As you stitch, you will want the main portion of the stitch to lie on the appliqué fabric, with one edge of the stitch just barely dropping off the edge of the appliqué fabric into the background fabric.

The Stitching Process

To avoid a nasty thread ball on the back of your work, bring the bobbin thread up through all the layers.

1. With the top thread held above (and free of) the presser foot, lower the presser foot.

2. Use the hand wheel on your machine to make one complete stitch (your machine might have a button that will do this automatically), with the take-up lever started *and* stopping in the highest position.

3. Tug gently on the tail of the top thread. A loop of bobbin thread should pop up through the layers.

4. Pull the end of the bobbin thread through to the top layer. Hold both threads under the presser foot and out of the way as you start to stitch.

5. Continue holding both the top and bobbin threads until you have locked your stitches. You can go back and clip these threads later.

6. Secure your stitching. You can use a locking stitch (several stitches almost on top of each other) or a stop stitch if your machine has one, or you can stitch back and forth in place, creating a small bar tack.

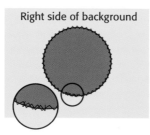

Right side of background

7. Stitch around your appliqué shape, ending again with a locking stitch or small bar tack. If you are stitching around an enclosed shape, overlap the beginning and ending of your stitching by about ⅜".

If you find you are veering off the edge of your appliqué, don't panic! Simply reverse your stitching to get back to where you were last on target, and then start stitching in a forward direction again. One of the advantages of using the .004 monofilament is that the extra stitching usually doesn't show on the front of your work!

ASSEMBLING THE BODY OF THE QUILT

Some of the projects in this book are made in the medallion style, with a series of borders surrounding a single block. Others feature pieced units assembled in a vertical-strip style. Several are classic block-style patterns, arranged either in a straight set or diagonally.

In each case, arrange the blocks as shown in the photograph and diagram provided for each project. Press the seam allowances in the directions recommended. For the quilts using a vertical-strip style, you will generally press the seam allowances toward the bottom of the quilt. For the block-style quilts, you will press seams in opposite directions from row to row so that the intersections will nest when the rows are sewn together. For diagonally set quilts, add the corner triangles last.

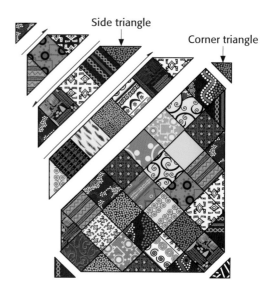

Side triangle

Corner triangle

Press the final set of seams in one direction, usually toward the bottom of the quilt.

ADDING BORDERS

Sometimes you'll find that you prefer the way your project looks without adding a border, or you might feel that it would look better with a narrower or wider border than I have indicated. Follow your heart! Whatever you decide, I suggest that you not cut any border fabrics until the body of your quilt is complete. Fabrics sometimes behave in rather unpredictable ways when they are combined; the border fabric you thought was perfect may suddenly not look right at all! Variations in seam allowances, or even in pressing, affect the finished size of a quilt top, so it is always best to measure the body of your own quilt top to determine the dimensions needed, rather than relying solely on mathematical calculations.

The yardage requirements for the border fabrics in this book assume that you will make butted (not mitered) borders, with wide outer borders for bed-sized quilts or throws cut on the lengthwise (parallel to selvage) grain of the fabric for extra stability. To conserve fabric, yardage requirements for narrow inner borders or for borders on small projects assume that the border strips will be cut on the crosswise grain, from selvage to selvage.

When you need to make a long inner-border strip, join the strips with a diagonal seam to reduce bulk.

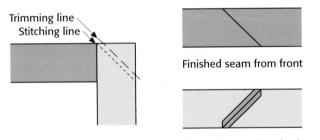

Trimming line
Stitching line

Finished seam from front

Finished seam from back

The following steps describe the process of adding borders:

1. The width of the border strips will be listed in the instructions for each project. To determine the total length you will need, measure your quilt top from top to bottom. Take this measurement through the center of the quilt, since the outer edges may have stretched slightly during handling.

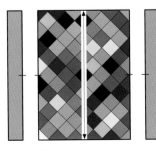

Measure center of
quilt, top to bottom.
Mark centers.

When pinning border strips to your quilt top, pin the middle of the strip first, and then either end. The next pins should go between the end and the middle points. Continue dividing up the space between pins until the border is secure. Pinning the border in this manner prevents the border strip from stretching or scooting down the quilt top as you sew, plus it evenly distributes any excess fullness.

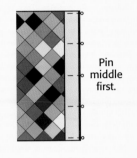

Pin middle first.

2. If necessary, join inner-border strips with a diagonal seam to arrive at the length you need.

3. Sew the side borders to the quilt top, and press the seam allowances away from the body of the quilt. Next, measure the new width of the quilt top with the side borders added. Cut the top and bottom borders to this measurement, and sew them to the top and bottom of the quilt top. Press the seam allowances away from the body of the quilt.

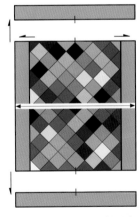

Measure center of quilt, side to side, including border strips. Mark centers.

4. If you have more than one border on your project, sew the first border fabric to all four sides of the quilt top before adding the next border fabric.

5. Repeat steps 1 through 4 for each additional border.

African and Australian Squares on Point

This fun (and super quick to make) quilt showcases a wonderful assortment of African and Australian fabrics.

MATERIALS

With the exception of the fat quarters, yardage is based on 42"-wide fabric.

1¾ yards total of assorted fabrics for blocks and corner triangles

¾ yard total (or 5 fat quarters) of fabric for side triangles

⅜ yard of fabric for inner border

1⅞ yards of fabric for outer border

3¼ yards of fabric for backing (pieced horizontally)

⅝ yard of fabric for binding

56" x 72" piece of batting

CUTTING

From the assorted fabrics for blocks and corner triangles, cut:
   61 squares, 6" x 6"; cut 2 squares once diagonally

From the fabric for side triangles, cut:
   5 squares, 10½" x 10½"; cut each square twice diagonally

From the inner-border fabric, cut:
   5 strips, 2" x 42"

From the outer-border fabric, cut:
   6 strips, 5" x *length of fabric*

From the binding fabric, cut:
   7 strips, 2½" x 42"

Note: This pattern features the "cut them big" approach to side and corner triangles. This will create a small space between the outer points of the squares and the seam of the inner border, giving the impression that the blocks are "floating."

FAT QUARTER FRIENDly!

By Kerry Steinberg, 2001, Grand Rapids, Michigan. 51⅞" x 67⅜".

ASSEMBLING THE BODY OF THE QUILT

1. Referring to the project photo and diagram, lay out 59 blocks, side triangles, and corner triangles on the diagonal as shown.

2. Sew side triangles to appropriate blocks. With right sides together, align the corner of each triangle with the corner of the adjacent square. Stitch a seam. Trim the excess point after pressing.

 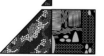

3. Working on the diagonal, sew the blocks into rows. Press the rows in alternate directions.

4. Sew the rows together; the seam allowances between blocks should nest at the intersections.

5. Sew corner triangles to the quilt top. Press toward the corners.

6. Use a rotary cutter, ruler, and cutting mat to trim away the fabric at the edges of the quilt top. The quilt shown was trimmed ⅞" from the tips of the blocks.

⅞"

FINISHING

1. As described in "Adding Borders" on page 24, measure the inner and outer borders and sew them to the quilt, always pressing the seam allowances away from the quilt center.

2. Layer and baste the quilt top, batting, and backing fabric as described in "Basting the Quilt Sandwich" on page 70.

3. Quilt as desired. The project shown was quilted in the ditch between squares and along the border seams. Free-motion quilting was added in the outer border as described in "Hand-Guided (Free-Motion) Quilting" on page 72.

4. Square up the quilt sandwich as described in "Squaring Up" on page 73.

5. Prepare the binding and sew it to the quilt. See "Binding" on page 75 for detailed instructions.

6. Sign and date your work, and enjoy your creation!

Australian Rail Fence

Aboriginal fabrics from Australia breathe new life and vigor into this adaptation of a traditional North American quilt pattern.

MATERIALS

Yardage is based on 42"-wide fabric.

For Block A:

Fabric 1	¾ yard (**Note:** This is combined yardage for blocks A and B.)
Fabric 2	⅜ yard
Fabric 3	½ yard
Fabric 4	½ yard

For Block B:

Fabric 5	⅜ yard
Fabric 6	⅝ yard
Fabric 7	½ yard

Also:

1¾ yards of fabric for border

3 yards of fabric for backing (pieced horizontally)

½ yard of fabric for binding

51" x 66" piece of batting

CUTTING

Number and width of strips:

Fabric 1	13 strips, 1¾" x 42"
Fabric 2	6 strips, 1½" x 42"
Fabric 3	6 strips, 2¼" x 42"
Fabric 4	6 strips, 2" x 42"
Fabric 5	7 strips, 1½" x 42"
Fabric 6	7 strips, 2¼" x 42"
Fabric 7	7 strips, 2" x 42"

From the border fabric, cut from the lengthwise grain:

4 strips, 4" wide

From the binding fabric, cut:

6 strips, 2½" x 42"

DESIGN DECISIONS: DIRECTIONAL FABRICS

The striped Australian fabrics used in this quilt were printed with the strips running perpendicular to the selvages instead of parallel to them. Since I wanted to feature the flashes of curvy cream stripes against the dark backgrounds as a major design element, I needed to cut my strips on the lengthwise grain instead of on the cross grain, as is customary. Therefore I needed extra yardage of those fabrics: 44" (or 1⅛ yards) each of fabric 2 for block A and fabric 5 for block B.

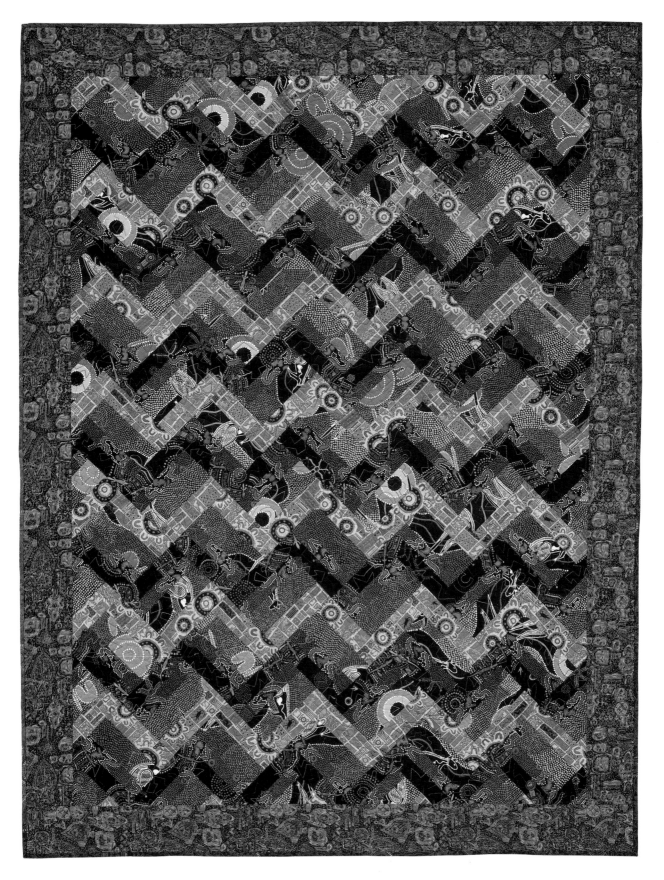

Designed by Beth Ann Williams, made by Mary Kuras, 2002, Grand Rapids, Michigan. 46¼" x 61¾".

MAKING THE BLOCKS

1. As directed in "Sewing Strip Sets" on page 19, sew six identical strip sets for block A. Press all the seam allowances toward the bottom strip in each strip set.

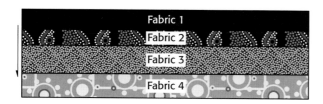

2. From these strip sets, cut 39 blocks, 6" square.

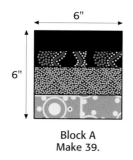

Block A
Make 39.

Note: Measure your strip sets; they should measure exactly 6" wide. If they are consistently wider or narrower than 6", use this personal measurement when cutting all your blocks—they need to be square!

3. As directed in "Sewing Strip Sets" on page 19, sew seven identical strip sets for block B. Press all the seam allowances toward the bottom strip in each strip set.

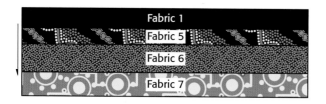

4. From these strip sets, cut 44 blocks, 6" square (or, again, whatever dimension exactly matches the width of your strip sets).

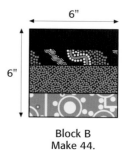

Block B
Make 44.

ASSEMBLING THE BODY OF THE QUILT

1. Lay out the blocks as shown.

2. Working on the diagonal, sew the blocks into rows. Press rows in alternate directions.

3. Sew the rows together. The seam allowances between blocks should nest at the intersections. Press all seams in one direction.

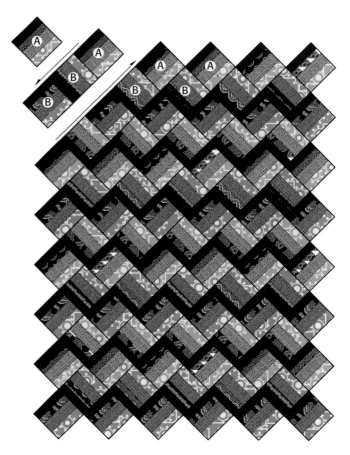

4. Use a rotary cutter, ruler, and cutting mat to trim away the extra fabric at the edges of the quilt. Align your ruler with the points of the blocks and trim, leaving a ¼" seam allowance.

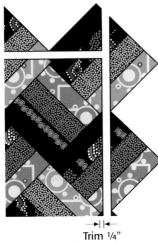

→| |←
Trim ¼"
from point.

FINISHING

1. As described in "Adding Borders" on page 24, measure the border and sew it to the quilt, always pressing the seam allowances away from the quilt center.

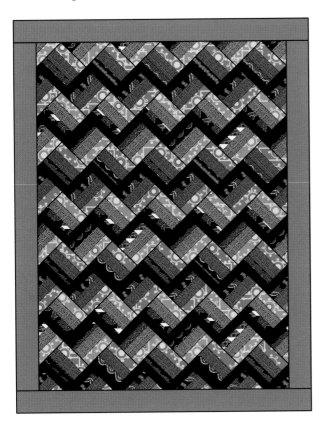

2. Layer and baste the quilt top, batting, and backing fabric as described in "Basting the Quilt Sandwich" on page 70.

3. Quilt as desired. The project shown was free-motion quilted in an allover pattern as described in "Hand-Guided (Free-Motion) Quilting" on page 72.

4. Square up the quilt sandwich as described in "Squaring Up" on page 73.

5. Prepare the binding and sew it to the quilt. See "Binding" on page 75 for detailed instructions.

6. Sign and date your work, and enjoy your creation!

BACK STORY

Bush Tucker, a fabric that appears in two different colorways in "Australian Rail Fence," depicts a wide variety of bush tucker (food) motifs such as goannas, snakes, witchetty grubs, and wiry seeds. Animal and human tracks are also included, as is a camp with people sharing food. (*Information courtesy of Leo9 Textiles.*)

Bush Tucker fabric by Sarah Nelson
© Stirling Station.

African Coins

Memories of open-air market stalls piled high with colorful fabrics provided the inspiration for this design.

MATERIALS

With the exception of the fat quarters, yardage is based on 42"-wide fabric.

⅛ yard (or 1 fat quarter) each of 49 fabrics for multicolored columns

¾ yard of black-and-white print fabric for geometric columns

⅝ yard of black fabric for geometric columns

2⅜ yards of black fabric for vertical sashing strips and borders

5½ yards of fabric for backing (pieced vertically)

¾ yard of fabric for binding

71" x 90" piece of batting

CUTTING

From *each* of the fabrics for multicolored columns, cut:
   1 strip, 2" x 42" (If using fat quarters, you will need 2 strips, 2" x 21".)

From the black-and-white print fabric, cut:
   17 strips, 1¼" x 42"; crosscut 10 strips into 108 rectangles, 1¼" x 3½"

From the black fabric for geometric columns, cut:
   7 strips, 2¾" x 42"

From the black fabric for sashing strips and borders, cut on the lengthwise grain:
   8 strips, 2" wide (sashing strips)
   2 strips, 5" wide (side borders)
   2 strips, 6½" wide (top and bottom borders)
   Save remaining fabric for filler pieces.

From the binding fabric, cut:
   9 strips, 2½" x 42"

FAT QUARTER FRIENDLY!

By Beth Ann Williams, 2002, Grand Rapids, Michigan. Quilted by Nancy Roelfsema. 67" x 86".

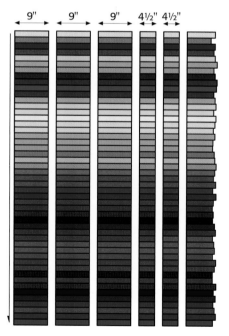

MAKING THE MULTICOLORED COLUMNS

1. Arrange the 49 strips as desired. Label them and sew them into a strip set as described in "Sewing Strip Sets" on page 19. If using fat quarters, you will need two identical strip sets.

2. With your strips horizontal, fold the strip set carefully and align the bottom fold with a line on your cutting mat.

3. From this strip set cut three segments, 9" wide, and two segments, 4½" wide. Or, if using fat quarters, cut two 9" segments from the first strip set, and from the second strip set cut one 9" segment and two 4½" segments.

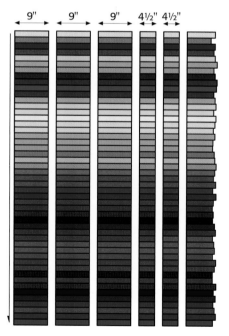

9"   9"   9"   4½" 4½"

Cut 3 segments 9" wide and 2 segments 4½" wide.
You will have a small segment left over.

MAKING THE GEOMETRIC PIECED COLUMNS

1. Sew seven strip sets combining the 1¼" black-and-white print strips with the 2¾" strips of black. Press seams toward the black fabric. Crosscut the strip sets into 104 segments, 2½" wide.

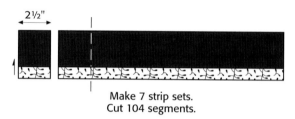

2½"

Make 7 strip sets.
Cut 104 segments.

2. Lay out and assemble the geometric columns with 26 strip-set segments in each column. Sew a 1¼" x 3½" black-and-white print rectangle between each strip-set segment. Sew a rectangle to the top and bottom of each column as well. Press the seam allowances toward the bottom of each column.

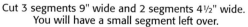

Make 2.

Make 2.

3. Measure the length of your multicolored columns. Cut black filler strips and sew them to both ends of each geometric column so that all columns are the same measurement.

Note: Mathematically these filler pieces should be cut ⅞" x 6½", but your dimensions may vary slightly. Use your leftover pieces of vertical sashing to cut these pieces.

ASSEMBLING THE BODY OF THE QUILT

1. Lay out the body of the quilt, alternating the multicolored columns, black vertical sashing strips, and geometric pieced columns as shown.

2. Sew the vertical columns together, pressing all seam allowances toward the black sashing strips.

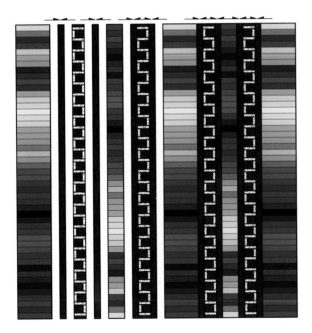

FINISHING

1. As described in "Adding Borders" on page 24, measure the borders and sew them to the quilt, always pressing the seam allowances away from the quilt center.

2. Layer and baste the quilt top, batting, and backing fabric as shown in "Basting the Quilt Sandwich" on page 70.

3. Quilt as desired. The project shown was quilted by Nancy Roelfsema in an allover pattern incorporating a wide variety of African-inspired shapes and symbols.

4. Square up the quilt sandwich as described in "Squaring Up" on page 73.

5. Prepare the binding and sew it to the quilt. See "Binding" on page 75 for detailed instructions.

6. Sign and date your work, and enjoy your creation!

DESIGN DECISIONS

Since I am an enthusiastic collector of African fabrics (and a long-term member of Unique Spool's African Fat Quarter Club), I jumped at the chance to use as many different African fabrics as I could. However, it is not really necessary to accumulate that much fabric in order to make this quilt!

You can also achieve a terrific look with just seven fabrics. Make two identical strip sets, with each set repeating the fabrics seven times. A fat quarter of each fabric should still provide sufficient yardage.

Shield

Handmade shields are still used by hunters in many parts
of Africa. This version is my own "protective" design.

MATERIALS

*With the exception of the fat quarters, yardage is based on
42"-wide fabric.*

¼ yard each of 9 African fabrics for quilt center

⅝ yard each of 2 different animal prints for borders

½ yard of contrasting print for triangle accents in
borders

2½ yards of fabric for backing (pieced horizontally)

½ yard of fabric for binding

44" x 56" piece of batting

Freezer paper

CUTTING

From *each* of the 9 African fabrics, cut:
2 strips, 3" x 42"

From *each* of the prints for borders, cut:
4 strips, 5" x 42"

From the triangle-accent fabric, cut:
1 square, 13" x 13"; crosscut twice diagonally

From the binding fabric, cut:
5 strips, 2½" x 42"

MAKING THE QUILT CENTER

1. You will need two strip sets (or four half-length
   sets if you are using fat quarters), using one of
   each of the nine African-fabric strips per set.
   Arrange your fabrics as shown in the illustration, with the lightest fabric first. In the quilt
   shown, the first five fabrics are arranged light to
   dark (starting with the lightest fabric in the
   quilt) and the next four fabrics are arranged
   medium to dark. Label and sew the strip sets as
   described in "Sewing Strip Sets" on page 19.
   Press the seams of strip set 1 *away* from the first
   strip; press the seams of strip set 2 *toward* the
   first strip.

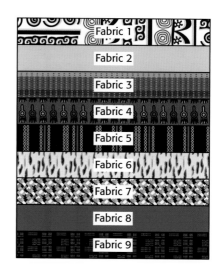

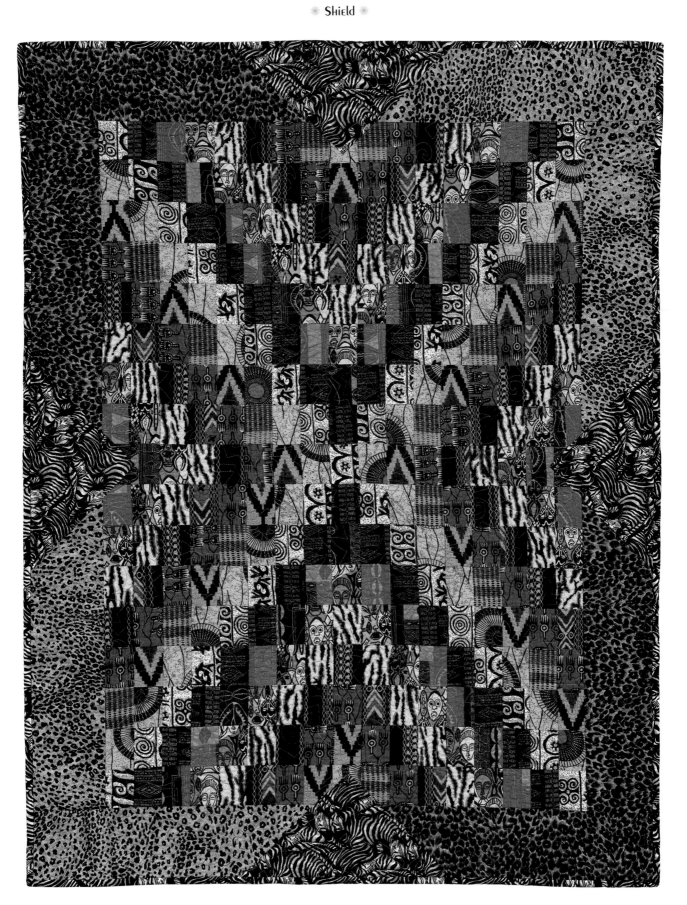

By Beth Ann Williams, 2001, Grand Rapids, Michigan. 39¼" x 52".

2. Create a tube out of strip set 1 by sewing the unsewn long edge of the first strip to the unsewn edge of the last strip. Sew with right sides together. Repeat with strip set 2. Label them 1 and 2.

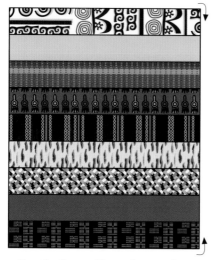

Sew the first and last strips together.

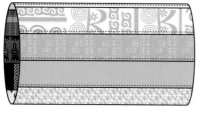

Make 2.

3. For the top half of the quilt, cut nine 2¼"-wide loops from tube 1 and eight 2¼"-wide loops from tube 2.

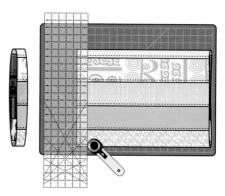

4. Open up a loop from tube 1 by unpicking the seam so that the lightest fabric is at the top of the segment.

It will be easier to unpick the seams to open your loops if you use a contrasting color in your bobbin. To open a seam, slit the bobbin thread every 4 to 5 stitches. Turn the fabric over and you should be able to pull the top thread out all in one piece.

5. Open up a loop from tube 2 so that the lightest fabric has moved down one position.

6. Continue alternating tubes and opening up loops until the lightest fabric has moved to the bottom position. Repeat until the lightest fabric has returned to the top position. Alternating tubes in this manner will allow your seam allowances to oppose each other, making them much easier to match up than if they had all been pressed in the same direction.

7. To keep your segments in order while you sew, number them with masking tape. Sew the segments together, and press all seams in one direction.

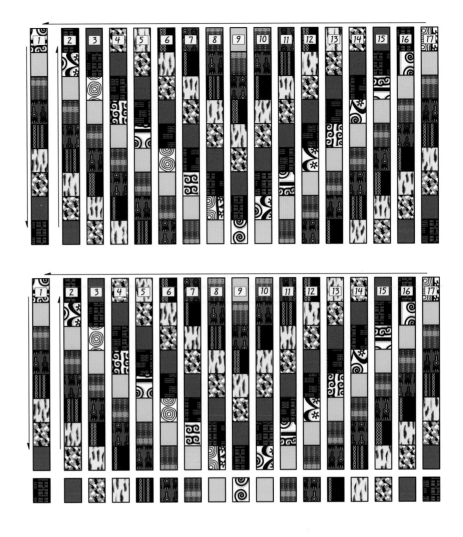

8. To create the lower half of the quilt, repeat steps 3–7, except this time remove the bottom fabric after each loop is opened. Label the segments and sew them in order. Press all seams in the same direction as the top half.

   Note: If you run out of fabric from the first tube, you can cut the needed segment from the second tube; just remember to press the seams in the opposite direction before using it.

9. To complete the design, rotate the lower panel and sew it to the bottom of the upper panel. Seams will nest against each other.

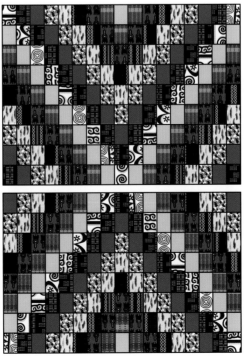

ADDING THE BORDERS

To create the unique border shown, two different fabrics are used on each side of the quilt.

1. Measure the center section of the quilt from top to bottom through the middle.

2. Sew one strip of border fabric A *end to end* to border fabric B. Press the seam allowance toward the darker fabric.

3. Trim the border strip to the measurement obtained in step 1, being careful to keep the seam centered. Along the left side of the quilt, align the border seam with the center of the quilt.

4. Pin and sew the border strip to the quilt. Press the seam allowance away from the quilt center.

5. Repeat steps 2–4 for the right side of the quilt, being careful to position the border fabrics as shown in the diagram below.

6. Measure the center section of the quilt from side to side, including the border you just added.

7. Repeat steps 2–4 for the top and bottom of the quilt, again referring to the diagram for fabric placement.

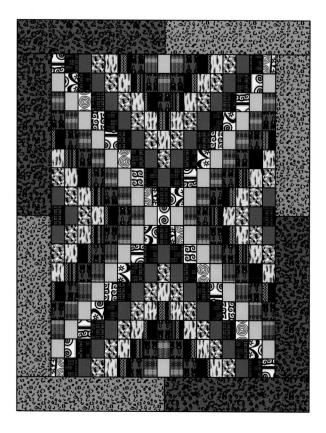

8. Cut one 12" square of freezer paper twice diagonally to create the four templates needed for the accent triangles at the quilt edges.

9. Following the procedure described in "Invisible Machine Appliqué" on page 22, press the short edges of the triangle fabric over the edges of the freezer paper, but trim the long edge of the triangle fabric even with the template.

10. Pin the triangles in place, aligning the tip of each triangle with the center of each edge of the quilt, covering the seam between the two border fabrics. Align the raw edges of the triangles with the raw edges of the borders.

11. Appliqué the sides of the triangles in place.

12. Reaching in through the open edge of each triangle, use your fingernail to pull the seam allowance away from the freezer paper and pull the paper out.

FINISHING

1. Layer and baste the quilt top, batting, and backing fabric as shown in "Basting the Quilt Sandwich" on page 70.

2. Quilt as desired. The project shown was free-motion quilted in an allover pattern consisting mainly of geometric fill, as described in "Hand-Guided (Free-Motion) Quilting" on page 72.

3. Square up the quilt sandwich as described in "Squaring Up" on page 73.

4. Prepare the binding and sew it to the quilt. See "Binding" on page 75 for detailed instructions.

5. Sign and date your work, and enjoy your creation!

BACK STORY: IN THIS CASE, LITERALLY!

I used a wonderful Masai print designed by Kaye England for the backing of this quilt. I felt that the fabric not only fit perfectly with the theme of the quilt, but the print was also so great that I was reluctant to cut it up and lose the bold impact of the design. The solution—a reversible quilt!

African-Inspired Backing Fabric of "Shield," Designed by Kaye England

JAPANESE INDIGOS

*The indigo fabrics used in this quilt are all from Hanamomen of Japan;
the red border fabric is from Moda's Chinese-themed "Year of the Dragon."*

MATERIALS

Yardage is based on 42"-wide fabric.

½ yard each of 6 light-valued indigo fabrics for blocks

½ yard each of 6 medium-to-dark-valued indigo fabrics for blocks

⅞ yard of small-scale red print for sashing

2⅝ yards of large-scale red print for top and bottom borders

9 yards of fabric for backing (pieced vertically)*

⅞ yard of fabric for binding

89" x 99" piece of batting

Depending on the width of your fabric, you may need only 6 yards.

CUTTING

From *each* of the light and medium-to-dark indigo fabrics, cut:
    2 strips, 7½" x 42". Divide the strips into 2 identical groups, so that no fabric is repeated within the same group.

        From each strip in the first group, cut:
            4 rectangles, 7½" x 9½" (for 48 total)

        From each strip in the second group, cut:
            3 rectangles, 7½" x 9½" (for 36 total)
            1 rectangle, 7½" x 5½" (for 12 total)

From the small-scale red print fabric, cut:
    17 strips, 1½" x 42"; crosscut into 84 rectangles, 1½" x 7½"

From the large-scale red print fabric, cut from the lengthwise grain:
    2 strips, 10" wide

From the binding fabric, cut:
    10 strips, 2½" x 42"

DESIGN DECISION

Jewel-toned cotton sarong fabrics in Indonesian batiks (see photo on page 9) would be stunning in this pattern, as they are very similar in scale to the Japanese indigos. A golden-brown sarong batik could easily take the place of the red prints used here for sashing and borders.

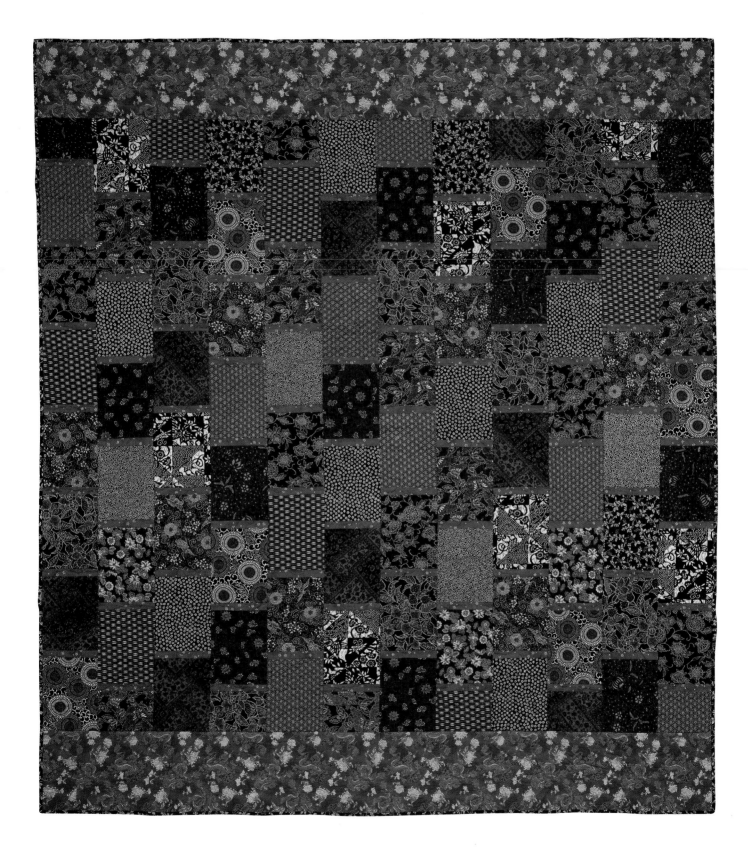

By Beth Ann Williams and Carolyn Eary, 2002, Grand Rapids, Michigan.
Quilted by Debra Becker. 84½" x 94½".

ASSEMBLING THE BODY OF THE QUILT

1. Arrange the blocks in rows as shown. Each vertical row will either begin or end with a partial block (a 7½" x 5½" rectangle). Each full block and partial block is separated from its neighbor by a red sashing strip.

2. Sew the blocks and sashing strips together into vertical rows. Press all seam allowances toward the bottom of each row.

3. Sew the rows together. Press these seam allowances all in the same direction.

FINISHING

1. As described in "Adding Borders" on page 24, measure and sew the top and bottom border strips, always pressing the seam allowances away from the quilt center.

2. Layer and baste the quilt top, batting, and backing fabric as shown in "Basting the Quilt Sandwich" on page 70.

3. Quilt as desired. The project shown was machine quilted on a long-arm machine by Debra Becker, who used an allover pattern she adapted from a flower found in one of the dark indigo fabrics. The pattern she used is on page 47.

4. Square up the quilt sandwich as described in "Squaring Up" on page 73.

5. Prepare the binding and sew it to the quilt. See "Binding" on page 75 for detailed instructions.

6. Sign and date your work, and enjoy your creation!

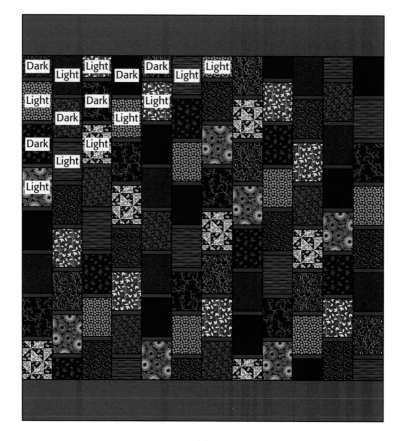

Start

Finish

Continuous Line Quilting Design

Noshi

This quilt takes both its inspiration and its name from the Japanese tradition of Noshi (see "Back Story" on page 51).

MATERIALS

Yardage is based on 42"-wide fabric.

Block A:

Fabric 1 (light)	¼ yard
Fabric 2 (dark)	¼ yard
Fabric 3 (dark)	¼ yard
Fabric 4 (light)	¼ yard
Fabric 5 (light)	¼ yard
Fabric 6 (dark)	⅜ yard
Fabric 7 (dark)	⅜ yard
Fabric 8 (light)	¼ yard
Fabric 9 (light)	⅜ yard
Fabric 10 (dark)	½ yard
Fabric 11 (dark)	½ yard
Fabric 12 (light)	⅜ yard
Fabric 13 (light)	⅜ yard
Fabric 14 (dark)	½ yard
Fabric 15 (dark)	¾ yard

Block B:

Fabric 16 (light)	¼ yard
Fabric 17 (dark)	¼ yard
Fabric 18 (dark)	¼ yard
Fabric 19 (light)	¼ yard
Fabric 20 (light)	¼ yard
Fabric 21 (dark)	⅜ yard
Fabric 22 (dark)	⅜ yard
Fabric 23 (light)	¼ yard

Block B (continued):

Fabric 24 (light)	⅜ yard
Fabric 25 (dark)	½ yard
Fabric 26 (dark)	½ yard
Fabric 27 (light)	⅜ yard
Fabric 28 (light)	⅜ yard
Fabric 29 (dark)	½ yard
Fabric 30 (dark)	¾ yard

Also:

¾ yard of fabric for inner border

2¾ yards of fabric for outer border

8¼ yards of fabric for backing (3 widths/pieced horizontally)

⅞ yard of fabric for binding

96" x 107" piece of batting

Note: I numbered the fabrics up to 30 because 30 different fabrics can be used to make the blocks. However, the quilt shown did not use 30 fabrics. Instead, we arranged fabrics 1 through 15 in a different order for each block. To do this, you'll simply need to double the listed yardage amounts for each of the first 15 fabrics. Using two different colorations of the same off-center Log Cabin block, as in the following instructions, will prevent the sometimes jarring effect that can occur when two logs of the same fabric end up next to each other in your final quilt layout.

Designed by Beth Ann Williams, made by Nancy Roelfsema,
2002, Grand Rapids, Michigan. 92" x 102½".

CUTTING

For Block A (make 28):

Fabric	Number/width of strips to cut	Log size (x28)
Fabric 1 (light)	2 strips, 2" x 42"	2" x 2"
Fabric 2 (dark)	2 strips, 2" x 42"	2" x 2"
Fabric 3 (dark)	3 strips, 2" x 42"	2" x 3½"
Fabric 4 (light)	3 strips, 1½" x 42"	1½" x 3½"
Fabric 5 (light)	4 strips, 1½" x 42"	1½" x 4½"
Fabric 6 (dark)	4 strips, 2" x 42"	2" x 4½"
Fabric 7 (dark)	5 strips, 2" x 42"	2" x 6"
Fabric 8 (light)	5 strips, 1½" x 42"	1½" x 6"
Fabric 9 (light)	6 strips, 1½" x 42"	1½" x 7"
Fabric 10 (dark)	6 strips, 2" x 42"	2" x 7"
Fabric 11 (dark)	7 strips, 2" x 42"	2" x 8½"
Fabric 12 (light)	7 strips, 1½" x 42"	1½" x 8½"
Fabric 13 (light)	7 strips, 1½" x 42"	1½" x 9½"
Fabric 14 (dark)	7 strips, 2" x 42"	2" x 9½"
Fabric 15 (dark)	10 strips, 2" x 42"	2" x 11"

For Block B (make 28):

Fabric	Number/width of strips to cut	Log size (x28)
Fabric 16 (light)	2 strips, 2" x 42"	2" x 2"
Fabric 17 (dark)	2 strips, 2" x 42"	2" x 2"
Fabric 18 (dark)	3 strips, 2" x 42"	2" x 3½"
Fabric 19 (light)	3 strips, 1½" x 42"	1½" x 3½"
Fabric 20 (light)	4 strips, 1½" x 42"	1½" x 4½"
Fabric 21 (dark)	4 strips, 2" x 42"	2" x 4½"
Fabric 22 (dark)	5 strips, 2" x 42"	2" x 6"
Fabric 23 (light)	5 strips, 1½" x 42"	1½" x 6"
Fabric 24 (light)	6 strips, 1½" x 42"	1½" x 7"
Fabric 25 (dark)	6 strips, 2" x 42"	2" x 7"
Fabric 26 (dark)	7 strips, 2" x 42"	2" x 8½"
Fabric 27 (light)	7 strips, 1½" x 42"	1½" x 8½"
Fabric 28 (light)	7 strips, 1½" x 42"	1½" x 9½"
Fabric 29 (dark)	7 strips, 2" x 42"	2" x 9½"
Fabric 30 (dark)	10 strips, 2" x 42"	2" x 11"

From the inner-border fabric, cut:
8 strips, 2½" x 42"

From the outer-border fabric, cut on the lengthwise grain:
4 strips, 7½" wide

From the binding fabric, cut:
10 strips, 2½" x 42"

MAKING THE BLOCKS

To avoid confusion, work on just one set of blocks at a time.

1. To create the A blocks, sew log 1 (a light fabric) to log 2 (a dark fabric). Press the seam allowance toward the darker fabric.

2. As shown in the block A illustration, add log 3 (a dark fabric). Always press the seam allowances toward the most recently added log.

3. Continue to work your way around in a counterclockwise manner, adding a log to each side as you turn the block, ending with log 15 (a dark fabric).

4. Make 28 identical A blocks.

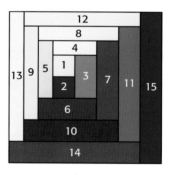

Block A

5. Repeat to make 28 identical B blocks.

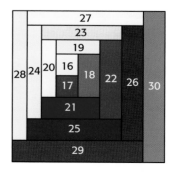

Block B

ASSEMBLING THE BODY OF THE QUILT

1. Lay out the blocks in eight horizontal rows of seven blocks each, alternating blocks A and B and rotating them to create the pattern shown.

2. Sew the blocks together into rows, pressing seam allowances in each row in the same direction and alternating direction from row to row. Sew the rows together. Press seam allowances toward the bottom of each row.

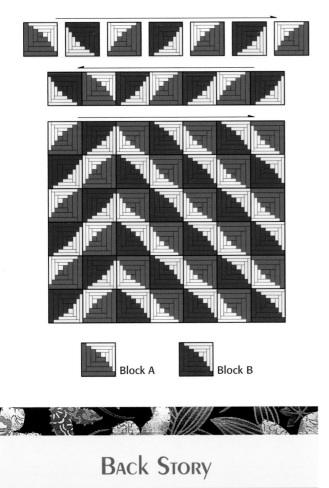

Block A   Block B

BACK STORY

The word *noshi* means "to expand" or "to prosper." Noshi is represented artistically as a bundle of long strips gathered (usually tied) in the middle. Originally, Noshi was made of abalone, a shellfish, and was offered to the gods. On auspicious occasions such as New Year's Day, weddings, or feast days, gifts were wrapped with a strip of Noshi attached. Now Noshi is more commonly represented in paper.

FINISHING

1. As described in "Adding Borders" on page 24, measure the inner and outer borders and sew them to the quilt as shown at right, always pressing the seam allowances away from the quilt center.

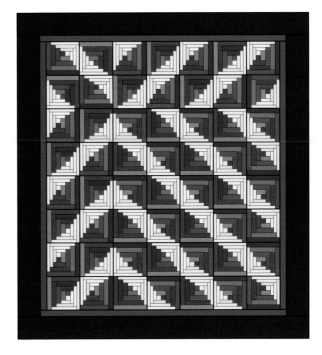

2. Layer and baste the quilt top, batting, and backing fabric as shown in "Basting the Quilt Sandwich" on page 70.

3. Quilt as desired. The project shown was free-motion quilted by Nancy Roelfsema in a swirling allover pattern as described in "Hand-Guided (Free-Motion) Quilting" on page 72.

4. Square up the quilt sandwich as described in "Squaring Up" on page 73.

5. Prepare the binding and sew it to the quilt. See "Binding" on page 75 for detailed instructions.

6. Sign and date your work, and enjoy your creation!

Adinkra Pillow

This pillow features batik squares stamped with Adinkra symbols, which originated in Ghana, West Africa. The elephant "nine patches" are actually squares fussy cut from a design that was screen-printed by hand. The fabric, from Zimbabwe, was purchased through Magie Relph.

MATERIALS

With the exception of the fat quarters, yardage is based on 42"-wide fabric.

4 Adinkra-painted blocks at least 4½" square (Mine came from Indonesian Batiks, but you could also use embroidered or printed fabric squares.)

¼ yard of fabric for alternate squares

⅛ yard of fabric for inner border

¼ yard of fabric for outer border

⅝ yard of fabric for lining

⅝ yard of fabric for backing

21" x 21" piece of batting

18" pillow form

Note: I prefer to use a pillow form that is slightly larger than the pillow cover to make a nice, plump pillow!

FAT QUARTER FRiENDly!

DESiGN DECiSiONS

Many African fabrics are printed either in stripes or block-style. These offer great opportunities to get more "bang for your buck." By fussy cutting squares from the elephant fabric, I was able to create the illusion of pieced blocks instead of plain squares.

By Beth Ann Williams, 2002, Grand Rapids, Michigan. 16¾" x 16¾".

CUTTING

Trim the Adinkra blocks (if necessary) to 4½" x 4½".

From the fabric for alternate squares, cut:
1 strip, 4½" x 42"; crosscut into 5 squares,
4½" x 4½" (See "Design Decisions" on page 52.)

From the inner-border fabric, cut:
2 strips, 1¼" x 42"

From the outer-border fabric, cut:
2 strips, 2½" x 42"

From the lining fabric, cut:
1 square, 20" x 20"

From the backing fabric, cut:
2 rectangles, 13½" x 17½"

MAKING THE PILLOW TOP

1. Lay out the nine center squares as shown.

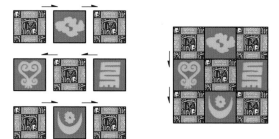

2. Sew each row, pressing all seams in each row in the same direction, and alternating the direction from row to row.

3. As described in "Adding Borders" on page 24, sew the inner and outer borders to the pillow. Press all border seams away from the center.

4. Make a quilt sandwich by layering first the lining, then the batting, and finally the pillow top. Pin to keep the layers from shifting, or use fusible batting.

5. Stitch in the ditch between the squares and in each border seam, as described in "Machine-Guided (Walking-Foot) Quilting" on page 71. Add a line of echo quilting in the outer border (optional).

ASSEMBLING THE PILLOW

1. With your rotary cutter, ruler, and cutting mat, trim the quilted pillow top to 17½" x 17½".

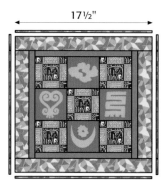

2. On the wrong side of each backing piece, turn one long raw edge over twice to form a ⅜"-wide hem. Press. Topstitch the folds to finish them.

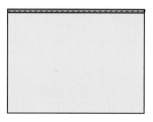

3. Place the quilted pillow top and one hemmed panel right sides together, aligning the long unfinished edge of the backing panel with the top raw edge of the pillow top.

4. Place the remaining hemmed backing panel right sides together with the quilted pillow top, this time aligning the long unfinished edge of the backing panel with the bottom raw edge of the pillow top. The hemmed edges of the two backing panels will overlap.

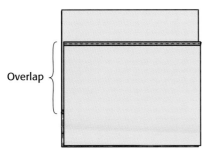

Overlap

5. Pin generously. Stitch completely around the outside edge of the pillow top using a ⅜"-wide seam allowance. Reinforce the hemmed edges of the pillow back by stitching over those areas three times. Trim the corners at an angle to reduce bulk.

6. Use a zigzag stitch (or a serger) to finish the raw edges of the seam around the pillow. (This prevents the fabric from raveling when the pillow cover is washed.)

7. Turn the pillow cover right side out. Insert the pillow form, carefully poking out the corners and smoothing the pillow covering to eliminate lumping or bunching.

BACK STORY: Adinkra Symbols

Although the symbols I used for this pillow were actually made in Indonesia, Adinkra cloth was developed around the eighteenth century by the people of Ghana, in West Africa. Originally reserved for royal and spiritual leaders and for important sacred ceremonies, *adinkra* means "good-bye," and was worn for mourning. Now it is incorporated into a wide range of social activities, including churchgoing, festivals, weddings, naming ceremonies, and initiation rites. The Republic of Ghana has a wonderful Web site explaining Adinkra symbols, each of which has a name and meaning derived from a proverb, historical event, human attitude, animal or plant life, or even an inanimate or man-made object.

The meanings of the symbols used in the pillow are as follows:

Top: "bite not one another," "avoid conflicts," UNITY

Left: "no taboo to return and fetch what you forgot," "undo mistakes," LEARN FROM THE PAST

Right: "changing oneself," "playing many roles," GROWTH

Bottom: "the moon and stars," FAITHFULNESS

Asian Fans Wall Hanging

A neat no-fail trick for producing lovely points combines with invisible machine appliqué for a quilt that's as fast as it is fun to make.

MATERIALS

With the exception of the fat quarters, yardage is based on 42"-wide fabric.

¾ yard of fabric for background

4 to 8 fat quarters of Asian-print fabric for fan blades (the more variety you have, the more interesting your project will be) **OR** assorted strips of Asian-print fabric at least 7" wide, totaling at least ½ yard

⅛ yard of fabric for fan and medallion centers

⅜ yard of fabric for inner border

⅝ yard of fabric for outer border

1⅛ yards of fabric for backing

⅜ yard of fabric for binding

38" x 38" piece of batting

Freezer paper

Fat Quarter Friendly!

CUTTING

From the background fabric, cut:
1 square, 24" x 24"

From each of the Asian-print fabrics, cut:
1 strip, 7" wide

From the inner-border fabric, cut:
4 strips, 2" x 42"

From the outer-border fabric, cut:
4 strips, 4" x 42"

From the binding fabric, cut:
4 strips, 2½" x 42"

Each 7" strip cut from a fat quarter will yield 6 to 7 fan blades. You will need a total of 24 blades to complete the design. However, to create the most pleasing combinations of color and texture, it is usually helpful to have additional selections on hand. I suggest using a minimum of four fabrics for the fans. I love variety, so I used many more!

By Beth Ann Williams, 2001, Grand Rapids, Michigan. 34" x 34".

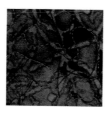

MAKING THE FANS

1. Trace the template provided on page 61 onto the dull side of a piece of freezer paper or other template material. Cut it out exactly on the drawn line.

2. Align the top and bottom of the template, dull side up, with the top and bottom of a 7" strip of Asian-print fabric, right side up, and press in place with a warm iron to keep it from shifting.

3. Use your rotary cutter and ruler to cut the sides of the fan blade. Rotate the template 180° on the fabric strip to cut the next blade. Continue in this manner to cut a total of at least 24 fan blades.

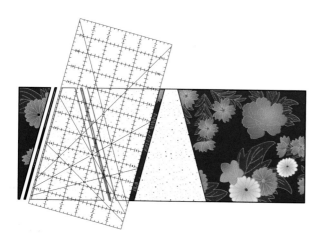

There are a couple ways you can maximize your efficiency while cutting the fan blades. I like to stack and cut three or four 7" strips of fabric at a time. Also, you can remove and reuse the freezer-paper template several times.

4. One at a time, pick up each fan blade and fold it in half lengthwise, right sides together. Stitch across the top (the wide end) of the folded blade. Without lifting the presser foot, place the next blade in position and sew across the top. Continue in this manner, chain piecing all 24 (or more!) of the fan blades.

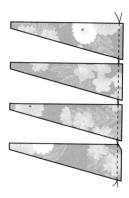

5. Cut the blades apart, and trim a small piece from the folded corner of each seam.

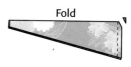

Fold

Trim corner by the fold.

6. Finger-press the seam open and turn the blade inside out so that the open seam is now flat and centered on the back side of the fan blade, creating a perfect point. You may need to use a point-turner or knitting needle to poke the point out all the way. Continue this process for the remaining blades.

Press seam open.

Turn and press flat.

7. Sew four sets of three blades each for the corner fans, pressing all seam allowances in one direction or, if you prefer, pressing them open to reduce bulk.

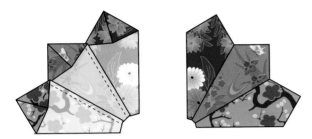

8. For the center medallion, sew two sets of six blades each. Press seam allowances to one side or, if you prefer, press them open to reduce bulk. Before sewing the two halves together, use your rotary cutter and ruler to sliver trim, if necessary.

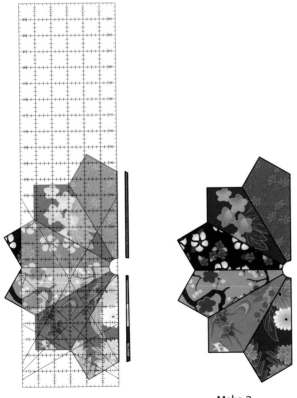

Make 2.

9. Sew the final seam to join the two halves, and press open.

ASSEMBLING THE WALL-HANGING TOP

1. Fold the 24" background square in half and press lightly (no steam). Unfold, and fold it in half the other way, again pressing lightly.

2. Use the fold lines on the background fabric to position the completed medallion in the center of the square, and pin in place.

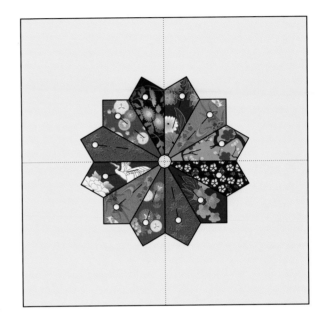

3. Appliqué the outer edge of the medallion with a small zigzag stitch and monofilament. Refer to "Invisible Machine Appliqué" on page 22 for details.

4. Pin a fan in each corner of the background square and appliqué in place.

5. Trace the larger circular template on page 61 onto the dull side of a piece of freezer paper. Cut the circle into quarters to create four identical pie shapes for the centers of the corner fans.

6. Once again drawing on the dull side of the freezer paper, trace and cut out the smaller circle on page 61 for the center of the medallion.

7. Prepare the centers and appliqué in place as described in "Invisible Machine Appliqué" on page 22.

8. Loosen the freezer paper from the edges of the seam allowance and pull out the templates from each of the four corner fans and corner quarter-circles.

9. Leaving a generous ¼" seam allowance, cut away a circle of background fabric from behind the medallion center. Loosen the edges of the seam allowance with your fingernail and pull out the template.

FINISHING

1. As described in "Adding Borders" on page 24, measure the inner and outer borders and sew them to the wall hanging, always pressing the seam allowances away from the center.

2. Layer and baste the wall-hanging top, batting, and backing fabric as shown in "Basting the Quilt Sandwich" on page 70.

3. Quilt as desired. The project shown was quilted in the ditch around the centers and outer edges of the fans and medallion, echo quilted just inside the outer edges of the fans and medallion, and in the ditch between the fan blades and along the border seams. Free-motion meandering was used in the background area and in the outer border.

4. Square up the quilt sandwich as described in "Squaring Up" on page 73.

5. Sew a display sleeve to the back of your wall hanging, referring to "Adding a Sleeve" on page 75.

6. Prepare the binding and sew it to the wall hanging. See "Binding" on page 75 for detailed instructions.

7. Sign and date your work, and enjoy your creation!

DESIGN DECISIONS

The large block that forms the center of this medallion-style wall hanging can also be used to make wonderful throws or bed quilts. Use four, six, or even nine blocks, depending on the size you need. You can add sashing between the blocks, or set them flush against each other. And don't forget the enlarging powers of borders!

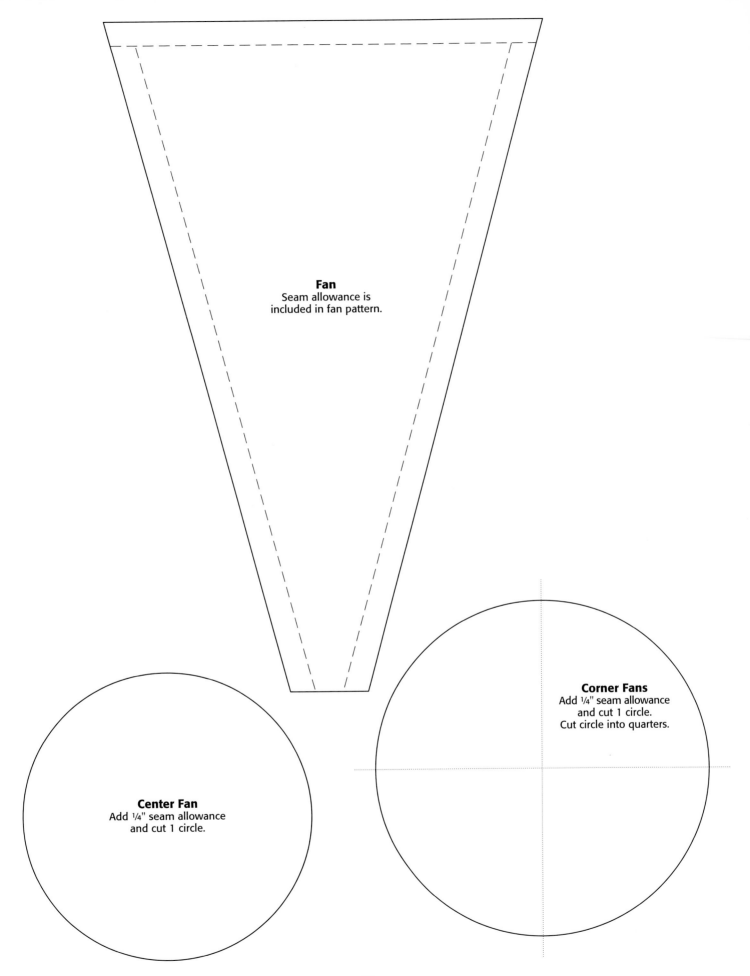

Fan
Seam allowance is
included in fan pattern.

Corner Fans
Add ¼" seam allowance
and cut 1 circle.
Cut circle into quarters.

Center Fan
Add ¼" seam allowance
and cut 1 circle.

Asian Fans Table Runner

My friend Nancy McCormick provided the inspiration behind this easy table runner, which would be equally suitable as an elegant wall hanging, especially in an entryway.

MATERIALS

With the exception of the fat quarters, yardage is based on 42"-wide fabric.

½ yard of fabric for background

4 to 8 fat quarters of Asian-print fabric for fan blades (the more variety you have, the more interesting your project will be) **OR** assorted strips of Asian-print fabric at least 6" wide, totaling at least ½ yard

⅛ yard of fabric for fan centers

⅛ yard of fabric for inner border

¼ yard of fabric for middle border

⅜ yard of fabric for outer border

1¼ yards of fabric for backing

⅜ yard of fabric for binding

25" x 44" piece of batting

Freezer paper

Fat Quarter Friendly!

CUTTING

From the background fabric, cut:
1 rectangle, 12½" x 32"

From each of the Asian-print fabrics, cut:
1 strip, 6" wide

From the inner-border fabric, cut:
3 strips, 1" x 42"

From the middle-border fabric, cut:
3 strips, 1½" x 42"

From the outer-border fabric, cut:
3 strips, 3" x 42"

From the binding fabric, cut:
4 strips, 2½" x 42"

Each 6" strip cut from a fat quarter will yield 8 to 9 fan blades. You will need a total of 32 blades to complete the design. However, to create the most pleasing combinations of color and texture, it is usually helpful to have additional selections on hand. I suggest using a minimum of four fabrics for the fans. I love variety, so of course I used more!

By Beth Ann Williams and Carolyn Eary, 2002, Grand Rapids, Michigan. 20½" x 40".

MAKING THE FANS

1. Trace the template provided on page 66 onto the dull side of a piece of freezer paper or other template material. Cut it out exactly on the drawn line.

2. Align the top and bottom of the template, dull side up, with the top and bottom of a 6" strip of Asian-print fabric, right side up, and press in place with a warm iron to keep it from shifting.

3. Use your rotary cutter and ruler to cut the sides of the fan blade. Rotate your template 180° on the fabric strip to cut the next blade. Continue in this manner to cut a total of at least 32 fan blades.

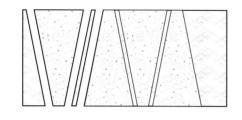

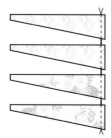

There are a couple ways you can maximize your efficiency while cutting the fan blades. I like to stack and cut three or four 6" strips of fabric at a time. Also, you can remove and reuse the freezer-paper template several times.

4. One at a time, pick up each fan blade and fold it in half lengthwise, right sides together. Stitch across the top (the wide end) of the folded blade. Without lifting the presser foot, place the next blade in position and sew across the top. Continue in this manner, chain piecing the fan blades.

5. Cut the blades apart, and trim a small piece from the folded corner of each seam.

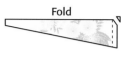

Fold

Trim corner by fold.

6. Finger-press the seam open and turn the blade inside out so that the open seam is now flat and centered on the back side of the fan blade, creating a perfect point. You may need to use a point-turner or knitting needle to poke the point out all the way. Continue this process for the remaining blades.

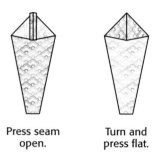

Press seam open.   Turn and press flat.

7. Sew two sets of four blades each for the corner fans, pressing all seam allowances in one direction or, if you prefer, pressing them open to reduce bulk.

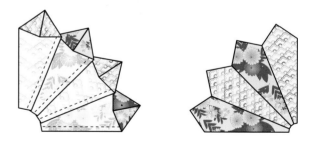

8. For the large side fans, sew three sets of eight blades each. Press seam allowances to one side or, if you prefer, press them open to reduce bulk.

ASSEMBLING THE TABLE-RUNNER TOP

1. Fold the background rectangle in half with short ends together; press lightly along the fold. Fold it in half again in the same direction and press the folds. You should have three equally spaced fold lines.

2. Use the fold lines on the background fabric to position the large side fans and pin in place. A fold line should pass through the center of each large fan.

3. Position the corner fans as shown and pin in place.

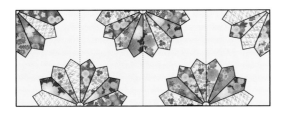

4. Appliqué the outer edge of each of the fans with a small zigzag stitch and monofilament. Refer to "Invisible Machine Appliqué" on page 22 for details.

5. Using the small circular template on page 66, trace two circles onto the dull side of a piece of freezer paper. Cut the circles in half to create four identical semicircles. (You will use only three.) These will be the centers for the side fans.

6. Once again drawing on the dull side of the freezer paper, trace and cut out the large circular template on page 66 for the corner fans. Cut the circle into quarters to create four pie shapes. (You will use only two.)

7. Prepare the centers and appliqué in place as shown in "Invisible Machine Appliqué" on page 22.

8. Loosen the freezer paper from the edges of the seam allowance and pull out the templates from each of the fans, semicircles, and quarter-circles.

FINISHING

1. As described in "Adding Borders" on page 24, measure the inner, middle, and outer borders and sew them to the table runner, always pressing the seam allowances away from the center.

2. Layer and baste the table-runner top, batting, and backing fabric as shown in "Basting the Quilt Sandwich" on page 70.

3. Quilt as desired. The project shown was quilted with feather stitching around centers and outer edges of the fans and along the border seams. The background area was free-motion quilted with a swirling allover pattern.

4. Square up the quilt sandwich as described in "Squaring Up" on page 73.

5. If desired, sew a display sleeve to the back of your quilt. See "Adding a Sleeve" on page 75.

6. Prepare the binding and sew it to the quilt. See "Binding" on page 75 for detailed instructions.

7. Sign and date your work, and enjoy your creation!

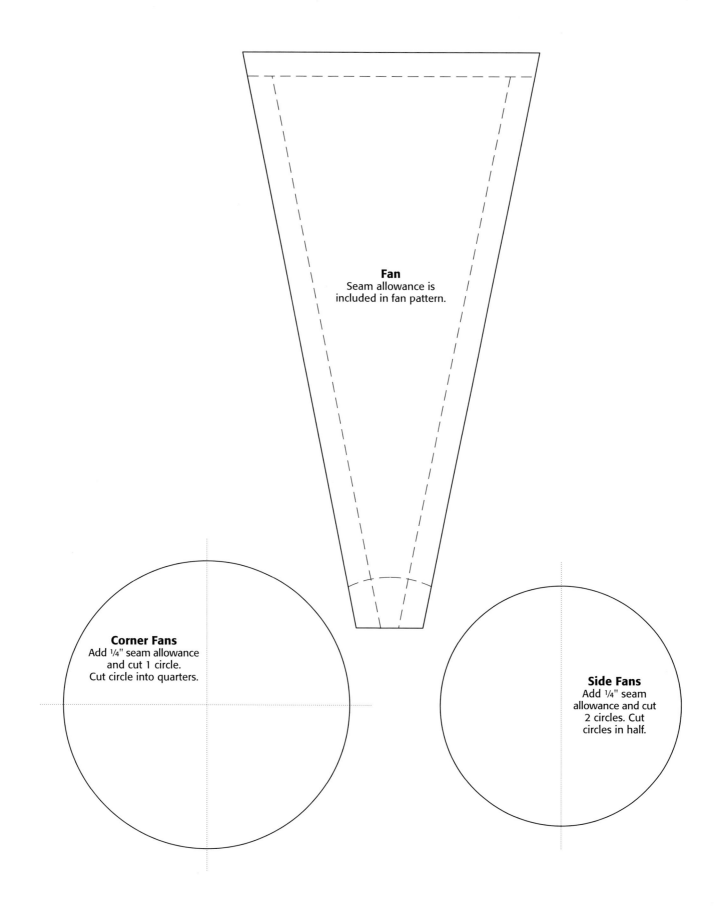

Fan
Seam allowance is
included in fan pattern.

Corner Fans
Add ¼" seam allowance
and cut 1 circle.
Cut circle into quarters.

Side Fans
Add ¼" seam
allowance and cut
2 circles. Cut
circles in half.

Undersea Grotto Wall Hanging

Hand-painted batik panels provide the focal points for this undersea adventure in fabric.

MATERIALS

With the exception of the fat quarters and panels, yardage is based on 42"-wide fabric.

3 batik panels at least 8" square

For the blocks (3):

Fabric 1	⅛ yard
Fabric 2	⅛ yard
Fabric 3	⅛ yard
Fabric 4	⅛ yard
Fabric 5	⅛ yard
Fabric 6	¼ yard

Also:

1⅜ yards of fabric for border

1½ yards of fabric for backing

⅜ yard of fabric for binding

23" x 50" piece of batting

CUTTING

Trim the painted batik panels (if necessary) to 8" square.

Note: If you prefer, you can use an embroidery machine to make your own fish designs, or simply cut panels from some of the great fish fabrics currently available.

From the block fabrics, cut:

Fabric	Number/width of strips to cut	Log size (x6)
Fabric 1	2 strips, 1½" x 42"	1½" x 8"
Fabric 2	2 strips, 1½" x 42"	1½" x 10"
Fabric 3	2 strips, 1½" x 42"	1½" x 10"
Fabric 4	2 strips, 1½" x 42"	1½" x 12"
Fabric 5	2 strips, 1½" x 42"	1½" x 12"
Fabric 6	3 strips, 1½" x 42"	1½" x 14"

From the border fabric, cut from the lengthwise grain:
3 strips, 3" wide

From the binding fabric, cut:
4 strips, 2½" x 42"

FAT QUARTER FRIENDLY!

By Beth Ann Williams, 2002, Grand Rapids, Michigan. 19" x 46".

MAKING THE BLOCKS

Except for the centers, all three of the blocks will be identical.

1. Sew a log 1 unit to opposite sides of each painted panel. Press seam allowances away from the center square.

2. Add logs 2 through 6 in the same manner as shown, always pressing seam allowances away from the center panel.

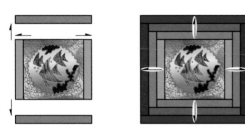

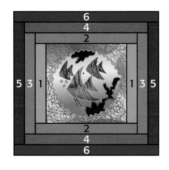

ASSEMBLING THE WALL-HANGING TOP

1. Sew the three blocks together as shown, pressing seam allowances toward the bottom of the wall hanging.

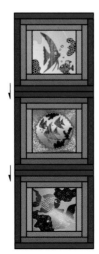

2. As described in "Adding Borders" on page 24, measure the borders and sew them to the wall hanging, always pressing the seam allowances away from the center.

FINISHING

1. Layer and baste the wall-hanging top, batting, and backing fabric as shown in "Basting the Quilt Sandwich" on page 70.

2. Quilt as desired. The project shown was free-motion quilted with spirals and crescents, as described in "Hand-Guided (Free-Motion) Quilting" on page 72, adding to the illusion of swirling ocean currents.

3. Square up the quilt sandwich as described in "Squaring Up" on page 73.

4. Sew a display sleeve to the back of your wall hanging, referring to "Adding a Sleeve" on page 75.

5. Prepare and sew the binding to the quilt. See "Binding" on page 75 for detailed instructions.

6. Sign and date your work, and enjoy your creation!

DESIGN DECISIONS

This wall hanging would be particularly nice livening up a small space. Alternatively, the three blocks could be finished and hung separately as a triptych, or made into pillows.

Finishing Techniques

Once you have completed the body of your quilt and added any borders, you are ready to turn your project into a quilt. Before you can start quilting, you will need to create a quilt sandwich consisting of the quilt top, batting, and backing fabric. Whether you choose to quilt by hand or by machine, these layers will need to be securely basted together so that they do not shift when you start quilting. When the quilting is complete, you will need to square up your project and bind it (or turn it into a pillow). If your quilt is destined to become a wall hanging, you'll probably want to add a sleeve to the back before you bind it.

BASTING THE QUILT SANDWICH

For machine quilting, pin basting is an easy and efficient way to hold the layers together. Unless I am using the new fusible batting by Hobbs (see "Batting" on page 17), I generally prefer to baste my quilt sandwich with safety pins, usually placing them no further than 3" apart.

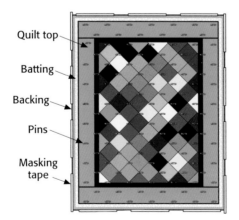

Quilt top
Batting
Backing
Pins
Masking tape

1. Press your quilt top and backing to remove any wrinkles or fold lines.

2. Lay the backing wrong side up on a clean floor or table.

3. Use wide masking or packing tape (check first to make sure that the tape you are using will not ruin the finish on your floor or table when you pull it up) to tape down all the edges, beginning with the centers of each side of the backing fabric and then the corners. Then, fill in around the entire perimeter of the quilt. The backing should be smooth and taut, but not stretched so tightly that the fabric becomes distorted.

4. Lay the batting on the backing and smooth it in place. The backing and batting should be 1"–2" larger all around than your quilt top. (This will give you something to hang on to when quilting and help prevent the border fabrics from stretching out of shape.)

As an alternative to tape, or if your quilt top is larger than your work area, you may also use clamps or binder clips to secure one or more edges of your backing fabric to a table or other supported work surface.

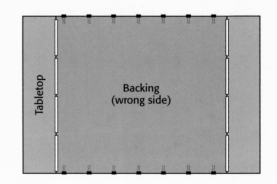

Tabletop

Backing (wrong side)

5. Smooth the quilt top into place. I like to use a ruler to double-check that my corners are square and that any straight lines in the quilt top are still straight.

6. Start pinning! I like to pin the outer edges first so that the border seams stay straight and I don't disturb or distort them when I reach (or crawl) over them to pin the interior area of the quilt. However, if you are concerned that you might end up with a bulge in the center, you can start pinning in the center and work outward. Pin the interior of the quilt in grid fashion with pins placed no more than 3" apart. Unless I need to crawl over some of the pins to reach other areas of the quilt, I like to wait until all the pins are in place before I close them.

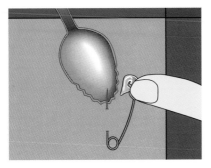

A grapefruit spoon is an effective tool for closing safety pins. The serrated edge helps keep the pin from slipping as you work.

MACHINE QUILTING VS. HAND QUILTING

Whether to quilt by hand or by machine is a matter of personal preference and aesthetic choice. For some of us, it may be determined by physical factors. Because of nerve damage in my hands and fingers, it is not practical for me to try to hand quilt. Fortunately, I discovered a long time ago that I like machine quilting for its speed, durability, and wonderful opportunities to add an additional layer of color and/or texture to my quilts. Since that is what I know best, the quilting instructions in this book are geared for machine quilting. For detailed information about hand-quilting techniques for both beginners and experts, my hand-quilting friends recommend Jeana Kimball's book *Loving Stitches: A Guide to Fine Hand Quilting* (That Patchwork Place, 1992) and Roxanne McElroy's book *That Perfect Stitch* (The Quilt Digest Press, 1998).

Several of the samples in the book were machine quilted by me on a regular home sewing machine. Kerry Steinberg quilted "African and Australian Squares on Point" and Mary Kuras quilted "Australian Rail Fence" on their home sewing machines; Nancy Roelfsema quilted "African Coins" and "Noshi" on her long-arm quilting machine; and Debra Becker quilted "Japanese Indigos" on her long-arm machine. Don't be alarmed by the amount of quilting you see on my quilts; it's really not necessary to quilt everything as heavily as I do. It's just that I enjoy machine quilting—especially free-motion quilting—and tend to go a bit overboard sometimes…

Note: Heavy machine quilting, especially in tandem with cotton or cotton-blend batting, can shrink the finished quilt quite a bit. My quilts tend to shrink several inches from the original size after quilting and washing.

There are two main categories of machine quilting. The first, machine-guided, relies on the feed dogs in your machine to keep the fabric moving through the machine as you stitch. The second, hand-guided, relies solely on your hands to move the fabric through the machine as you stitch—the needle will go up and down, but stitch length and direction are determined by how quickly and in what direction you move the fabric with your hands.

Machine-Guided (Walking-Foot) Quilting

Quilting in the ditch involves gently spreading the fabrics on either side of a seam apart and aiming for the seam or crevice between the two pieces. Because this stitching tends to be hidden when the fabric relaxes (especially after the quilt is washed), this is an especially forgiving method of machine quilting. For an even less-visible stitching line, many people like to use monofilament, but I also sometimes use cotton in a color that matches or blends with my fabrics.

Note: If you have pressed your seams open, you should not stitch in the ditch, as you will be stitching over the thread and potentially cutting through it. This can weaken your quilt.

Echo quilting involves stitching one or more lines parallel to previous lines of stitching. These lines may be spaced ¼" apart, ⅜" apart, or any other width you choose.

Channel quilting is straight-line quilting stitched in parallel rows. Attaching a quilting guide to your walking foot is an easy way to maintain consistent spacing between lines, or you can mark the fabric directly with chalk, soapstone, or a washable graphite marker.

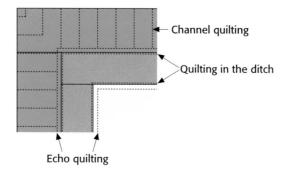

Channel quilting

Quilting in the ditch

Echo quilting

Don't overlook any decorative stitches built into your machine as a resource for creative machine quilting. The featherstitch is a favorite of mine—check it out on "Asian Fans Table Runner" on page 62.

Grid quilting can be effective for reinforcing a quilt that will be used heavily. Basically, it involves channel quilting in two directions. The lines can be at right angles to each other, forming a grid of squares, or they can form diamonds or hanging diamonds.

To set up your machine for machine-guided (walking-foot) quilting:

1. Attach your walking foot. (See the "Presser Feet" section on page 14 in "Equipment and Supplies.")

2. Leave the feed dogs up (the same position they are in for normal sewing).

3. If possible, lower the pressure on the presser foot slightly. For example, if a normal pressure setting for your machine is 3, try setting it back to 2 or 2.5; this will decrease the drag on the presser foot.

4. Set the stitch length to 10–12 stitches per inch (usually the default setting or the same setting you would use for most piecing).

5. Make a sample quilt sandwich to test and adjust (if necessary) the upper thread tension settings. Refer to #7 under "Beth Ann's Top Tips for Machine Quilting" on page 74.

6. Away you go! Well, almost. Before you begin sewing, see steps 1–6 of "The Stitching Process" on page 24, but instead of using a bar tack to secure the stitch, use a locking stitch or a very short stitch length (about 25 stitches per inch) at the beginning of the stitching line.

Hand-Guided (Free-Motion) Quilting

This type of machine quilting has been compared to hand quilting with an electric needle. The needle goes up and down in the machine, but nothing else moves unless you move it yourself. Stitch direction and stitch length are determined solely by how fast and in what direction you move the fabric with your hands. I like to think of it as drawing with my sewing machine. It's my favorite way to quilt!

Stippling, or the stitching that looks sort of like knobby puzzle pieces, is probably the best-known form of free-motion quilting, but there are as many different ways to free-motion quilt as there are quilters. Some people find that the wiggly motion of stippling or meandering (which is the same as stippling, just larger in scale) comes easily to them. Others may find it a bit frustrating, especially at first. But as I've taught machine quilting over the years, I have observed that almost every person can find some sort of free-motion patterning that comes more easily for her (or him) than others. I encourage you to set aside some time to doodle around on your sewing machine, seeing what kinds of lines feel most natural to you.

To set up your machine for hand-guided (free-motion) quilting:

1. Attach your darning foot. (See the "Presser Feet" section on page 14 in "Equipment and Supplies.")

2. Lower the feed dogs in your machine. If you cannot lower your feed dogs, you may have a throat plate or cover that snaps in place over them. I have found in my classes, however, that a cover often sticks up a bit and interferes with the functioning of the darning foot. If that is the case, it is generally best to leave the feed dogs

alone (with no cover) and simply set the stitch length almost to 0. This will reduce the movement of the feed dogs to a minimum. You might feel a little drag on the fabric, but the darning foot should still allow the fabric to move freely.

3. Set the pressure on the presser foot to 0 (if applicable to your machine).

4. Make a sample quilt sandwich to test and adjust (if necessary) the upper thread tension settings. Refer to #7 under "Beth Ann's Top Tips for Machine Quilting" on page 74.

5. Away you go! Well, almost. Before you begin sewing, see steps 1–6 of "The Stitching Process" on page 24, but instead of using a bar tack to secure the stitch, use a locking stitch or a very short stitch length (about 25 stitches per inch) at the beginning of the stitching line.

Here are some examples of various styles of free-motion quilting:

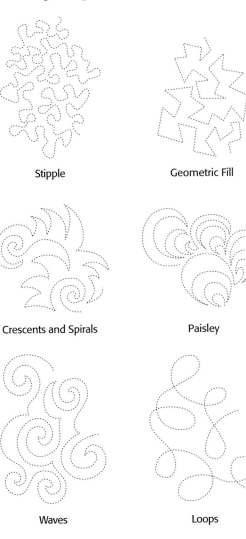

Stipple   Geometric Fill

Crescents and Spirals   Paisley

Waves   Loops

SQUARING UP

When you are finished with all the quilting, lay your project flat on your work surface (or clean floor). Smooth it out with your hands as best you can. Does it lie flat? If not, consider adding a bit more quilting in any area that is rippling or puffing up. You can also tame a limited amount of fullness by giving it a shot of steam and pulling it straight (let it cool completely before moving it) or by blocking the quilt after you wash it. Are the edges straight? Use your rotary-cutting ruler to make sure that the corners form a true 90° angle and that the quilt's edges are indeed straight. If they are not, you may need to sliver trim one or more edges with your rotary cutter.

Slide your cutting mat under the quilt, positioning it beneath those areas that need to be straightened. Don't worry about cutting into quilting lines; all the lines of stitching will be secured when you attach the binding.

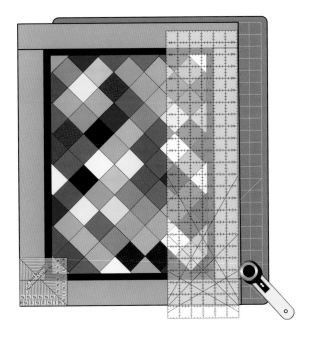

Measure the top and bottom of the quilt; the measurements should be equal. Do the same for the sides of the quilt.

Beth Ann's Top Tips for Machine Quilting

1. Try not to have any more than half of the quilt under the machine at any given time. In other words, if you are quilting straight lines across the quilt (such as stitching in the ditch along block or sashing seams), don't start at one end and simply work your way across the quilt. Instead, work from one direction for half of the quilt, then rotate it and work from the other direction for the remaining lines of stitching.

2. To isolate an area of the quilt for stitching, fold edges in loosely and secure the fold with three or four safety pins. (Rolling the quilt tends to create a very stiff, awkward tube, and I find that bicycle clips and other tools meant to secure the roll tend to get hung up on each other or hung up on the needle bar as I try to move the quilt through the machine.)

3. With a walking foot, *first* quilt any long, straight lines that go either all the way through the quilt or almost all the way through (between blocks, across major piecing lines, or along sashing or borders, for example). This stabilizes the quilt sandwich, and makes it easier to do any additional "fancy" quilting without causing the layers to shift.

4. Particularly on a bed-sized quilt, any designs (whether fancy motifs or stitching in the ditch around complicated pieced blocks) that involve multiple changes in direction are usually better done with a darning (or free-motion) foot. Any time you are rotating a large quilt while it is in your machine you risk layers sliding or bunching, especially right around the needle.

5. Work with your machine either in a cabinet or with an add-on table around it so that you have a flat working surface with plenty of room to support the quilt on either side of the machine. It is important that the weight of the quilt doesn't create drag (or stretch the quilt top) as it feeds through the machine toward the needle or past the needle.

6. Gloves with rubber grippers or rubberized fingers keep hands from slipping or skidding on fabric, improving control and reducing strain and fatigue.

7. If your bobbin thread is visible on the top of your work, your upper thread tension is too high and should usually be turned to a lower number. If your top thread is visible on the back of your work, and/or the bobbin thread feels very loose, your upper thread tension is too low and should usually be turned to a higher number. However, if you adjust your upper thread tension and your stitch does not improve, the issue is more likely that the machine should be unthreaded and rethreaded, and perhaps cleaned thoroughly. Winding your bobbin too quickly or at an uneven speed can also contribute to problems with thread tension.

8. Whatever style of quilting you do, remember to distribute the quilting evenly across the quilt; if one area is heavily quilted and another is not, it is unlikely that your finished quilt will lie flat.

9. When trimming the thread at the end of a line of stitching, first clip the top thread as close as you can to the surface of the quilt; then turn the quilt over and tug on the bobbin thread to pull the whisker of top thread into the batting. Hold the bobbin thread taut and clip it as close to the back of the quilt as possible. When the thread relaxes, it too will be drawn back into the batting.

10. As you stitch, remember to look ahead to where you are going next, not at the needle. (This may take some practice to build confidence in your hand-eye coordination; but consider how far you'd get driving a car if you spent the whole time staring at your hood ornament!)

11. BREATHE! And take *lots* of breaks—your arms, neck, and shoulders can get *very* sore, and the going gets really tough when you're in pain. But remember, this is supposed to be FUN!

ADDING A SLEEVE

Many quilt shows require a 3" to 4" hanging sleeve; I find that sleeves are handy for hanging pieces at home, also. My favorite display method is invisible from the front, with the quilt lying almost flush against the wall with no visible means of support.

1. Cut the sleeve the same length as the measurement of the top edge of the quilt, and 7" to 9" wide (depending on whether you want a 3" or 4" finished sleeve).

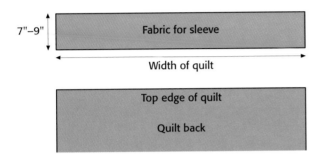

2. Fold both short edges under twice, about ⅜" each time, on the wrong side of the sleeve fabric; press. Topstitch the folds for a finished edge.

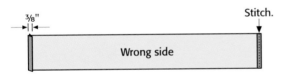

3. Fold the fabric in half lengthwise, right side out, and press. Pin the folded sleeve in place on the back of the quilt, matching the raw edges of the sleeve with the top raw edge of the quilt sandwich. The quilt should extend approximately ¾" beyond the sleeve at either end.

4. Stitch the top edge of the sleeve in place, using a scant ¼"-wide seam allowance. (This seam should be covered when you sew on the binding.)

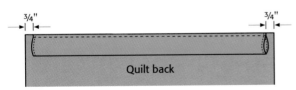

5. Hand stitch the remaining edges of the sleeve to the back of the quilt, making sure that your stitches do not show on the front of the quilt.

TIPS

❋ To hang a completed quilt at home, I take a 2½"- or 3"-wide wooden lattice or molding strip cut to the same length as the finished sleeve and add eyelet screws to either end. The eyelet screws hang on nails in my wall and are completely hidden behind the quilt between the edge of the hanging sleeve and the binding.

❋ If you are using wooden lattice strips, molding, or dowels, be sure to seal the wood before letting it come in contact with your quilt. This will protect the fabric from the acids in the wood. You can do this with varnish, paint, or even spray acrylic sealer.

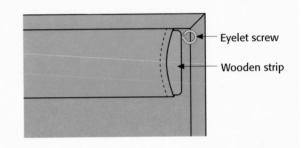

BINDING

I like to finish a quilt with a narrow French-fold binding, cut 2½" wide and finishing at ⅜" wide. Since the edges of the quilts in this book are all straight, you can cut the binding strips from selvage to selvage on the straight of grain instead of on the bias.

Prepare the Binding

1. To eliminate bulges in the finished binding, sew with a diagonal seam when joining binding strips.

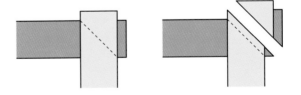

2. Press the seams open.

3. Fold the binding in half lengthwise with wrong sides together; press.

4. Open the binding strip at its starting end and fold the lower corner inward to create a 45° angle.

Fold line

5. Leaving a ¼"-wide seam allowance, trim away the tip of the triangle formed on the inside of the binding.

6. Refold the binding strip.

Machine Sew the Binding to the Quilt Front

1. Lay the binding around the quilt to make sure the seams of the joined binding strips will not fall on the corners of the quilt.

2. When are you satisfied with the placement, position the beginning of the binding (the triangular edge) on the right side of the quilt, with the raw edges of the binding even with the raw edges of the quilt sandwich. Do not begin at a corner.

3. Leaving the first 5" unsewn, stitch the binding to the right side of the quilt with a ⅜"-wide seam allowance. Use a walking foot to keep the binding from stretching as you sew.

4. Stop stitching ⅜" from the first corner.

5. With the needle down, pivot the quilt and stitch straight off the corner at a 45° angle.

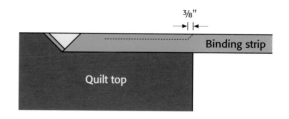

⅜"

Binding strip

Quilt top

6. Fold the binding strip up and away from the corner; then fold it back down and even with the next edge to create a pleat in the binding. Make sure the pleat is straight, and even with the edge of the quilt.

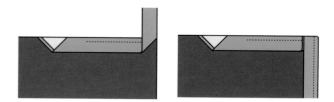

7. Holding the thread out of the way, slide the edge of the quilt back under the presser foot. Beginning right at the edge of the quilt, resume normal sewing.

8. Continue in the same manner around the remaining edges and corners.

9. Stop sewing several inches away from the starting point. Stop with the needle down, and keep the presser foot down as well.

10. Open the fold you made at the beginning of the binding, and tuck the end of the binding inside to determine how much excess length can be trimmed away.

11. On the diagonal, and in the same direction as the diagonal edge of the beginning of the binding (to avoid a bulky overlap), cut the extra fabric away from the end of the binding, making sure that the beginning and ending of the binding overlap about 1".

12. Tuck the end of the binding inside the fold at the beginning of the binding so that no cut edges are exposed.

13. Sew through all the layers, overlapping where you started stitching the binding at the beginning.

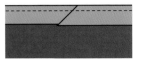

14. Turn the folded edge of the binding over the raw edge of the quilt and hand stitch it in place. The binding on the back of the quilt should cover the previous line of machine stitching that attaches the binding to the front of the quilt.

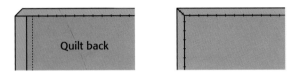

Quilt back

As you hand stitch the binding in place on the back of the quilt, keep your stitches from going through all the layers; you do not want them to show on the front of the quilt.

TIP

I find it easier to get perfectly flat mitered corners on my binding if I trim a tiny triangle from the corner of the quilt sandwich, reducing the bulk in that area.

Quilt back

WASHING AND BLOCKING

The first thing I do when I complete a quilt is wash it. Washing removes any stiffness, as well as dust, cat hair, and any other foreign matter. It also allows the stitching to sink down into the batting, creating a softer finished look. A quilt or other project that has been machine quilted with monofilament thread, in particular, looks much nicer after it has been washed. Methods for laundering quilts can be somewhat controversial, so use the method that works best for you!

Here are the washing steps that I take for my (non-antique) quilts:

1. Wash the quilt in the washer in cool water, on the gentle cycle. I like to use Synthrapol (a very mild detergent used in hand dyeing), Woolite Dye Magnet, or Shout Color Catcher sheets the first few times I launder a project (especially when incorporating fabrics from a variety of sources), just in case there is any residual dye migration.

2. Dry the quilt in the dryer on a gentle setting; if possible, take it out when it is still slightly damp.

3. Lay the quilt out to finish drying on a clean cotton blanket, mattress pad, or lint-free towel, making sure that the quilt is perfectly flat. If necessary, while the quilt is drying, lightly steampress and block any area that is uncooperative. You want the edges straight, the corners square, and the quilted areas free from distortion.

4. Allow the blocked quilt to cool and dry completely before disturbing it.

SIGNING AND LABELING YOUR FINISHED QUILT

Sign and date your work! You can write directly on the front or back of the quilt (or both) with a permanent, archival-quality, nonfading waterproof ink. (Scrapbooking pens are great!) You can also attach a permanent handwritten or computer-printed label to the back of your quilt. Consider including at least the following information: the title of the quilt (if applicable), the name of the quiltmaker, where the quilt was made, and the date it was completed. Additional information may include the inspiration behind the quilt, any special significance regarding the symbolism in the quilt, sources of special fabrics (especially souvenirs from world travels), or the person for whom the quilt was made. You'll be glad you did!

Bibliography
and Suggested Reading

Baird, Merrily. *Symbols of Japan: Thematic Motifs in Art and Design.* New York, NY: Rizzoli International Publications, Inc., 2001.

Clarke, Duncan. *The Art of African Textiles.* London: Thunder Bay Press, 1997.

Dower, John. *The Elements of Japanese Design: A Handbook of Family Crests, Heraldry & Symbolism.* New York & Tokyo: Weatherhill, Inc., 2000.

Dyrenforth, Noel. *The Technique of Batik.* London: B.T. Batsford Ltd., 1988/1997.

England, Kaye, and Mary Elizabeth Johnson. *Quilt Inspirations from Africa: A Caravan of Ideas, Patterns, Motifs and Techniques.* Lincolnwood (Chicago), Ill.: The Quilt Digest Press, 2000.

Gaudynski, Diane. *Guide to Machine Quilting.* Paducah, KY: American Quilter's Society, 2002.

Gillow, John. *Printed and Dyed Textiles from Africa.* Seattle, Wash.: University of Washington Press, 2001.

————. *Traditional Indonesian Textiles.* London: Thames & Hudson, Ltd., 1992.

Haigh, Janet. *Japanese Inspirations: 18 Quilted Projects.* Woodinville, Wash.: Martingale & Co., 2000.

Hargrave, Harriet, and Sharyn Craig. *The Art of Classic Quiltmaking.* Lafayette, Calif.: C&T Publishing, 2000.

Hargrave, Harriet. *Heirloom Machine Quilting: A Comprehensive Guide to Hand-Quilted Effects Using Your Sewing Machine.* Lafayette, Calif.: C&T Publishing, 1995.

Kimball, Jeana. *Loving Stitches: A Guide to Fine Hand Quilting.* Woodinville, Wash.: That Patchwork Place, 1992.

Kimura, Stephanie Masae. *Art to Wear with Asian Flair.* Iola, Wis.: Krause Publications, 2001.

Luke-Boone, Ronke. *African Fabrics: Sewing Contemporary Fashion with Ethnic Flair.* Iola, Wis.: Krause Publications, 2001.

McElroy, Roxanne. *That Perfect Stitch: The Secrets of Fine Hand Quilting.* San Francisco, Calif.: The Quilt Digest Press, 1998.

Noble, Maurine. *Machine Quilting Made Easy.* Woodinville, Wash.: That Patchwork Place, 1996.

Pahl, Ellen, editor. *The Quilter's Ultimate Visual Guide: From A to Z—Hundreds of Tips and Techniques for Successful Quiltmaking.* Emmaus, Penn.: Rodale, 1997.

Picton, John, and John Mack. *African Textiles, 2nd Ed.* London: British Museum Press, 1989.

Pippen, Kitty. *Quilting with Japanese Fabrics.* Woodinville, Wash.: Martingale & Co., 2000.

Shepard, Lisa. *African Accents: Fabrics and Crafts to Decorate Your Home.* Iola, Wis.: Krause Publications, 1999.

————. *Global Expressions: Decorating with Fabrics from Around the World.* Iola, Wis.: Krause Publications, 2001.

Shifrin, Laurie. *Batik Beauties: 18 Stunning Quilts.* Woodinville, Wash.: Martingale & Co., 2001.

Sudo, Kumiko. *Circles of the East: Quilt Designs from Ancient Japanese Family Crests.* Lincolnwood (Chicago), Ill.: The Quilt Digest Press, 1997.

Williams, Beth Ann. *Celtic Quilts: A New Look for Ancient Designs.* Woodinville, Wash.: Martingale & Co., 2000.

————. *Colorwash Bargello Quilts.* Woodinville, Wash.: Martingale & Co., 2001.

Yang, Sunny, and Rochelle M. Narasin. *Textile Art of Japan.* Tokyo: Shufunotomo/Japan Publications, 1989/2000.

Resources

Born to Quilt (online only)
Phone (toll-free): (877) 485-6320
Email: sales@borntoquilt.com
Web site: www.borntoquilt.com
(Wide selection of fabrics.)

Clotilde
PO Box 7500
Big Sandy, TX 75755-7500
Phone: (800) 772-2891
Fax: (800) 863-3191
Web site: www.clotilde.com
Free catalog available upon request.
(Excellent selection of notions and sewing supplies.)

Connecting Threads
PO Box 8940
Vancouver, WA 98668-8940
Phone: (800) 574-6454
Fax: (360) 260-8877
Web site:
www.ConnectingThreads.com
Free catalog available upon request.
(Wide selection of fabrics as well as notions.)

eQuilter.com
5455 Spine Rd., Suite E
Boulder, CO 80301
Phone: (877) FABRIC-3
or (303) 527-0856
Web site: www.equilter.com
(Wide selection of fabrics.)

Grand Quilt Co.
5290 Alpine Ave. NW
Comstock Park, MI 49321
Phone: (616) 647-1120
Fax: (616) 647-1074
Email: GrQuiltCo@aol.com
Web site: www.grandquilt.com
(Fabrics, notions, and local classes.)

Hancock's of Paducah
3841 Hinkleville Rd.
Paducah, KY 42001
Phone: (800) 845-8723
Web site:
www.Hancocks-Paducah.com
Free catalog available upon request.
(Wide selection of fabrics as well as notions.)

Indonesian Batiks
Vicki Hawkinson
14816 Hoxie Ln.
Anacortes, WA 98221
Phone: (360) 299-3968
Fax: (360) 299-1469
Web site: www.indobatiks.com
(Wide selection of batik art panels, including Adinkra symbols.)

Katie's Vintage Kimono
Katie Kendrick
PO Box 1813 Belfair, WA 98528
Phone: (360) 275-2815
Email: katienwalt@earthlink.net
Web site:
www.katiesvintagekimono.com
(Lovely kimono fabrics, including some cotton.)

Nancy's Notions
PO Box 683
Beaver Dam, WI 53916-0683
Phone: (800) 833-0690
Fax: (800) 255-8119
Web site: www.nancysnotions.com
Free catalog available upon request.
(Limited selection of fabrics, wide selection of notions and sewing supplies.)

Quilter's Junction
Phone (toll-free): (877) 998-2289
Email: quilt@quiltersjunction.com
Web site: www.quiltersjunction.com
(Selection of Langa Lapu hand-painted fabrics from South Africa, as well as other African, Australian, and Japanese fabrics.)

Salsa Fabrics (online only)
Phone: (775) 577-2207
Email: Chris@salsafabrics.com
Web site: www.salsafabrics.com
(Lovely selection of fabrics from Indonesia.)

St. Theresa Textile Trove, Inc.
1329 Main St.
Cincinnati, OH 45210
Phone: (800) 236-2450
Fax: (513) 333-0012
Email: info@sttheresatextile.com
Web site: www.sttheresatextile.com
(Wide selection of fabrics and embellishments.)

Unique Spool
407 Corte Majorca
Vacaville, CA 95688
Phone: (707) 448-1538
Email: spool@uniquespool.com
Web site: www.uniquespool.com
(Wonderful selection of fabrics from Africa, Australia, India, and the Pacific Rim; African Fabric Club offered.)

Outside the United States:
The African Fabric Shop
Magie Relph
19 Hebble Mount
Meltham West Yorkshire HD9 4HG
United Kingdom
Phone: 01484 850188
Web site: www.africanfabric.co.uk
(Wide range of fabrics from all over Africa.)

House of Patchwork
30 Tower Centre
Hoddesdon Herts EN11 8UB
United Kingdom
Phone: 44 01992 447544
Web site:
www.houseofpatchwork.co.uk
(Very nice selection of fabrics, notions, and sewing supplies.)

About the Author

Photo by Randall Nyhoff

Although born in the United States, Beth Ann Williams has spent a significant portion of her life in Africa and Europe. These life experiences have fostered a lifelong appreciation for the richness of varied historical, cultural, and artistic traditions. Beth is particularly fascinated by the interplay of color and value, symbolism, and how widely perceptions can differ both on individual levels and across cultures. She is also enthralled with the flow of line, and the formation of pattern—both natural and man-made.

Beth's quiltmaking pedigree, spanning generations, has gifted her with a profound respect for traditional approaches to the craft. However, she is best known for her innovative methods and more contemporary pieces. Her award-winning work has appeared in galleries, museums, books, magazines, and calendars. Individual pieces grace both public and private spaces.

Beth exhibits, lectures, and teaches workshops and classes nationally and internationally, as well as locally at Grand Quilt Company in Comstock Park, Michigan. She teaches in a variety of subject areas, including Celtic-style quiltmaking, bargello quilting techniques, decorative machine quilting, heirloom machine appliqué, impressionist-style piecing, abstract design, and color theory.

Beth holds a B.A. in communication arts from Cedarville University, Cedarville, Ohio. She is a member of the West Michigan Quilter's Guild, the Michigan Quilt Network, the National Quilting Association, the American Quilter's Society, the American Quilt Study Group, and the International Quilt Association.

She is the author of two other books published by Martingale & Company: *Celtic Quilts: A New Look for Ancient Designs* and *Colorwash Bargello Quilts.*

Beth lives in Grand Rapids, Michigan, with husband John Williams; their daughters, Caryl Elisabeth and Connor Marie; and two rather over-indulged cats, Chester and Charlie.